July 1993

Derivatives: Practices and Principles

Global Derivatives Study Group

Published by the Group of Thirty, Washington, DC

Foreword

This Study grew out of an informal meeting, convened last summer by the Group of Thirty, for those involved in financial derivatives activity. For some time, practitioners, regulators, and others concerned with the effective functioning and stability of financial markets had expressed to me their desire for an unofficial but authoritative review of industry practices and performance. In light of the Group of Thirty's past success in sponsoring work on important but technically abstruse financial questions, the Group appeared a natural place for launching such an effort.

I approached Dennis Weatherstone, Chairman of J.P. Morgan, and was delighted when he graciously agreed to lead a study. A broad cross-section of industry participants pledged their active support. Dennis promptly assembled a high-level Steering Committee with representatives from Europe, Japan, and North America. That Committee in turn established a similarly international and professionally diverse Working Group made up of senior managers and professionals from firms that are dealers and end-users, and from the related legal, accounting, and academic disciplines.

Their work proceeded separately from the continuing efforts of central bankers and other regulators to develop appropriate supervisory practices and capital requirements for the "off-balance-sheet" risks related to derivatives activity. Both perspectives, private and official, are obviously important. The hope and expectation of the Group of Thirty, in sponsoring this private study, is that the parallel tracks of inquiry will converge in market practices and regulatory approaches that complement each other.

From that perspective, the critically important contribution of this Study has been to define a set of sound risk management practices for dealers and end-users. The Recommendations and the Working Papers lay these out in detail. They also describe present practices. The Overview of Derivatives Activity clearly describes the nature of the activity and its potential for limiting and managing risk.

As private participants in derivatives activity, the authors of the Study deliberately intruded little on the domain of the regulators. That is perhaps most apparent in the virtual absence of comment about the appropriate level of capital requirements, an issue currently under regulatory review. Plainly, the authors believe that the amount of capital needed to support derivatives exposure is a matter of judgment for individual institutions, depending upon their appetite for risk and their ability to measure and manage it. That belief is not necessarily inconsistent with the view of regulators, who see the problem from a systemic perspective and conclude that certain minimum capital standards are appropriate as well.

The general attitude of the Study towards regulation is plain: derivatives by their nature do not introduce risks of a fundamentally different kind or of a greater scale than those already present in the financial markets. Hence, systemic risks are not appreciably aggravated, and supervisory concerns can be addressed within present regulatory structures and approaches. Where the official priority should be placed, in the view of the Study, is in clarifying legal uncertainties, and resolving legal inconsistencies between countries, that may impede risk-reduction procedures such as "netting."

This view may be subject to debate. But there can be no doubt that each organization's conscious and disciplined attention to understanding, measuring, and controlling risk along the lines suggested should help ensure that the risks to individual institutions and to markets as a whole are limited and manageable. To that end, the Study's first recommendation emphasizes the role of senior management.

The Recommendations for the management of derivatives activity have the unanimous endorsement of the Steering Committee. While the Study has been sponsored and supported by the Group of Thirty, I should note that, as with all our study group reports, it does not represent an official view of the Group. Nor does it necessarily represent the views of Group of Thirty members except those who served on the Steering Committee.

I gratefully acknowledge the intensive and careful effort that this document represents. Apart from the essential leadership of Dennis Weatherstone, the Working Group co-chairmen David Brunner, a Director of Paribas Capital Markets, and Patrick de Saint-Aignan, a Managing Director of Morgan Stanley, deserve special mention. To all those who participated, I would like to express the appreciation of the Group of Thirty.

I am confident that this Study will be required reading for those who take part in and supervise this large and important activity.

Paul Volcker
Chairman
Group of Thirty
July 1993

Group of Thirty Derivatives Project

Steering Committee

Chairman
Dennis Weatherstone
Chairman
J.P. Morgan

Members
Peter Cooke
Chairman
Regulatory Advisory
Practice
Price Waterhouse

Jessica Einhorn
Treasurer
World Bank

Rainer Gut
Chairman
Crédit Suisse

Toyoo Gyohten
Chairman
Bank of Tokyo

John Heimann
Chairman
Merrill Lynch Global
Financial Institutions

Thomas Johnson
Member
Group of Thirty

Yoh Kurosawa
President
Industrial Bank of Japan

Sir Peter Middleton
Deputy Chairman
Barclays Bank

Merton H. Miller
Professor
University of Chicago

Stephen Friedman
Chairman
Goldman Sachs & Co.

Eugene Shanks
President
Bankers Trust Company

Marc Viénot
Chairman
Société Générale

Edward Wauters
Chairman
Kredietbank NV

Working Group

Co-Chairmen
David Brunner
Director
Paribas Capital Markets

Patrick de Saint-Aignan
Managing Director
Morgan Stanley

Members
Malcolm P. Basing
President
Swiss Bank Corporation
Canada

Mark C. Brickell
Director
International Swaps and
Derivatives Association

Halsey Bullen
Project Manager
Financial Accounting
Standards Board

Michael Canby
Partner
Linklaters & Paines

Andrew Coleman
Partner
Capital Markets Group
Price Waterhouse

Daniel P. Cunningham
Partner
Cravath, Swaine & Moore

David Gelber
Chief Operating Officer
Midland Global
Markets/HSBC

Peter Hancock
Managing Director
J.P. Morgan

Tsuyoshi Hase
Senior Manager
Industrial Bank of Japan

James Healy
Managing Director
Credit Suisse Financial
Products

Judy Lewent
Vice President Finance, CFO
Merck Co., Inc.

Robert Mackay
Professor of Finance
Virginia Polytechnic Institute
and State University

Edson Mitchell
Senior Managing Director
Merrill Lynch

Daniel Mudge
Managing Director
Bankers Trust Company

Nancy Newcomb
Principal Financial Officer
Citicorp

Carleton D. Pearl
Vice President & Treasurer
McDonald's Corporation

Gary Perlin
Former Senior Vice President
& Treasurer
Fannie Mae

Kenneth Raisler
Special Counsel
Sullivan & Cromwell

S. Waite Rawls III
Executive Vice President
The Chicago Corporation

Ian Scott
Director of Treasury
Guinness PLC

Charles W. Smithson
Managing Director
The Chase Manhattan
Bank, N.A.

Charles Taylor
Executive Director
Group of Thirty

**Alexander
von Ungern-Sternberg**
Executive Vice President
Deutsche Bank

Akira Watanabe
General Manager
Mitsubishi Bank

Acknowledgments

In addition to the guidance of the Steering Committee and the efforts of the Working Group, the Group of Thirty gratefully acknowledges:

- The participation of respondents to the Survey of Industry Practice.

- The work of Price Waterhouse Capital Markets Group for conducting the Survey and providing the analysis of results.

- The work of the nine law firms who reviewed enforceability issues in different jurisdictions and, in particular, that of Cravath, Swaine & Moore, who organized this work and provided other support for the Study.

- The financial support of the following institutions:

American International Group

Bank of America

Bank of Tokyo

Bankers Trust Company

Banque Indosuez

Banque Paribas

Barclays Bank

Chase Manhattan Bank

Chemical Bank

Citicorp

Commerzbank

Crédit Suisse

CS First Boston

Dai-ichi Kangyo Bank

Daiwa Securities

Deutsche Bank

Dresdner Bank

Fidelity Investments

First Chicago

Fuji Bank

Goldman Sachs

HSBC Holdings

Industrial Bank of Japan

Kredietbank

Lloyds Bank

Merrill Lynch

Mitsubishi Bank

J.P. Morgan

Morgan Stanley

NatWest Markets

Nikko Securities

Nomura Securities

O'Connor & Associates

Price Waterhouse

Royal Bank of Canada

Sakura Bank

Salomon Brothers

Sanwa Bank

Société Générale

Standard Chartered

State Street Bank and Trust

Sumitomo Bank

Swiss Bank Corporation

Union Bank of Switzerland

S.G. Warburg Group

Yamaichi Securities

Table of Contents

Introduction

Introduction

Derivatives have fundamentally changed financial management by providing new tools to manage risk. As the use of derivatives has grown rapidly in the past 15 years, they have moved into the mainstream of finance.

Yet many, both inside and outside of the financial industry, remain uncomfortable with derivatives activity. They see it as complex and obscure, potentially subject to abuse that might lead to the failure of individual firms or even to a crisis in the financial system. This Study recognizes and addresses these concerns by explaining derivatives and their uses and by formulating and disseminating recommendations about their management.

The distinguishing feature of this Study is the practical character of its contents. Other studies of derivatives have been conducted by academics or supervisors; this Study was conducted largely by market participants.

Why Derivatives Matter

In general terms, a derivatives transaction is a contract whose value depends on (or "derives" from) the value of an underlying asset, reference rate, or index. This Study focuses on global "over-the-counter" (OTC) derivatives – those privately negotiated contracts provided directly by dealers to end-users, as opposed to the standardized contracts (such as futures) sold on exchanges. The main over-the-counter derivatives include swaps, forwards, and options, based upon interest rates, currencies, equities, and commodities.

By any measure, derivatives are a major financial activity. Some have even portrayed it as a multi-trillion dollar business dwarfing activity in other financial markets. But a more careful comparison reveals that, while derivatives activity is growing rapidly, its size remains modest in relation to foreign exchange, bonds, or equities.

What makes derivatives important is not so much the size of the activity, as the role it plays in fostering new ways to understand, measure, and manage financial risk. Through derivatives, the complex risks that are bound together in traditional instruments can be teased apart and managed independently, and often more efficiently.

The results can benefit a wide variety of institutions. For many that issue securities, and for many that invest, derivatives can save costs and increase returns while broadening the range of funding and investment alternatives. For them and others, derivatives can reduce the risk of loss. And for financial institutions, derivatives can be a source of strength because they reinforce existing activities with clients, and help to build diversified credit portfolios.

Derivatives and Risk

Derivatives help to manage risk in new ways – an important economic function. Yet the risks involved in derivatives activities are neither new nor unique. They are the same kinds of risks found in traditional financial products: market, credit, legal, and operational risks.

Because over-the-counter derivatives are customized transactions, they often assemble risks in complex ways. This can make the measurement and control of these risks more difficult and create the possibility of unexpected loss. Banking supervisors have conducted several studies into the implications of derivatives for the financial system. None of these studies concluded that derivatives significantly increase systemic risk, but neither did they find cause for complacency.

For derivatives activity to grow and prosper, those who take part in it – whether as dealers, end-users, or both – should continue laying a strong foundation of good management practice. They also should provide the public with information that will allay unjustified fears by demystifying this activity. And participants should discuss openly with legislators, supervisors, and regulators, ways to further strengthen the current institutional framework.

These steps are both appropriate and sufficient to address the systemic and other concerns about derivatives activity. Without minimizing the significance of these concerns, this Study does not conclude that any fundamental changes in the current regulatory framework, such as separate regulation of this activity, are needed. Separate regulation of global derivatives would be at cross-purposes with the existing framework of supervision, with its focus on the common risks contained in derivatives and traditional instruments. There is also a danger in imposing regulatory formulas that inhibit new product innovation or discourage firms from developing the individualized, robust risk management systems on which they should rely.

The Global Derivatives Study

This Study consists of the Recommendations, an Overview of Derivatives Activity, and three Appendices:

The Recommendations   The Study offers 20 recommendations to help dealers and end-users manage derivatives activity and continue to benefit from its use. The Study also recommends four ways that supervisors and regulators, for their part, can help the financial infrastructure keep up with derivatives activity.

The Overview of Derivatives Activity   The Overview section of this Study explains in relatively plain language what derivatives are, the needs they serve, their risks, and their relationship to traditional financial instruments. The Overview is intended to promote understanding and discussion among the growing number of people – in financial institutions, other corporations, and official bodies – that have an interest in the subject.

The Appendices   Three separately bound volumes of appendices contain the Study's detailed background material, which should be of special interest to professionals involved in various aspects of derivatives.

- Appendix I contains the six working papers that form the basis of the Study and whose analysis supports the Recommendations. Each covers one of the main areas studied by the Working Group: valuation and market risk; credit risk; enforceability; systems, operations, and controls; accounting and reporting; and systemic issues.

- Appendix II is a compilation of legal memoranda discussing issues of enforceability in nine jurisdictions: Australia, Brazil, Canada, England, France, Germany, Japan, Singapore, and the United States.

- Appendix III summarizes the findings of the Survey of Industry Practice conducted for this Study. A representative group of 80 dealers and 72 end-users responded to a detailed questionnaire.

By contributing to the public understanding of the nature and potential of derivatives, and by providing guidance on principles of good management, the authors of this Study hope to add to the soundness and utility of these instruments.

Recommendations

Recommendations
Contents

Recommendations

Summary

Global over-the-counter derivatives activity is relatively new, and until now there has been no thorough study of its management. Dealers and end-users, while aware of the broader challenges, have focused their discussions on specific issues – and have addressed these with a variety of practices, some more effective than others.

This Study presents the first comprehensive effort to take stock of what the industry has learned, and to broaden awareness of the more successful management approaches. It provides practical guidance in the form of 20 recommendations addressed to dealers and end-users alike (some firms perform both functions). These recommendations can help them to manage derivatives activity, to respond to its growth and complexity, and to continue to benefit from its use.

The recommendations, which the Steering Committee has endorsed unanimously, were formulated by the Working Group – a diverse cross-section of end-users, dealers, academics, accountants, and lawyers involved in derivatives. Input also came from a detailed Survey of Industry Practice among 80 dealers and 72 end-users worldwide, involving both questionnaires and in-depth interviews.

Some of the recommendations reflect a strong consensus among participants, and are already in widespread use; others represent the Working Group's choice among alternative practices. Still others point to emerging practices currently followed by a handful of participants.

These 20 recommendations are not necessarily the only means to good management. What they do offer is a benchmark against which participants can measure their own practices.

To summarize, the recommendations suggest that each dealer and end-user of derivatives should:

- *Determine at the highest level* of policy and decision making the scope of its involvement in derivatives activities and policies to be applied.

- *Value derivatives positions at market*, at least for risk management purposes.

- *Quantify its market risk* under adverse market conditions against limits, perform stress simulations, and forecast cash investing and funding needs.

- *Assess the credit risk* arising from derivatives activities based on frequent measures of current and potential exposure against credit limits.

- *Reduce credit risk by broadening* the use of multi-product master agreements with close-out netting provisions, and by working with other participants to ensure legal enforceability of derivatives transactions within and across jurisdictions.

- *Establish market and credit risk management functions* with clear authority, independent of the dealing function.

- *Authorize only professionals* with the requisite skills and experience to transact and manage the risks, as well as to process, report, control, and audit derivatives activities.

- *Establish management information systems* sophisticated enough to measure, manage, and report the risks of derivatives activities in a timely and precise manner.

- *Voluntarily adopt accounting and disclosure practices* for international harmonization and greater transparency, pending the arrival of international standards.

In addition, there are four recommendations for legislators, regulators, and supervisors. To help strengthen the financial infrastructure for derivatives activities, officials are called upon to:

- *Recognize close-out netting arrangements* and amend the Basle Accord to reflect their benefits in bank capital regulations.

- *Work with market participants to remove legal and regulatory uncertainties* regarding derivatives.

- *Amend tax regulations* that disadvantage the economic use of derivatives.

- *Provide comprehensive and consistent guidance* on accounting and reporting of derivatives and other financial instruments.

The recommendations are generally grouped below according to specific areas of study. Six subcommittees of the Working Group addressed these areas in detail. Their Working Papers, published separately as Appendix I, form the basis for these recommendations and provide essential background information.

Recommendations for Dealers and End-Users

These recommendations are addressed to participants in derivatives activity, both dealers and end-users. The terms "dealer" and "end-user" do not refer to particular types of institution, but rather to the nature of their derivatives activity. A bank, for instance, may participate both as a dealer and as an end-user. Likewise, some corporate end-users of derivatives may also be involved as dealers. (For information about who uses derivatives and why, see Section II of the Overview of Derivatives Activity.)

General Policies

Recommendation 1: The Role of Senior Management

Dealers and end-users should use derivatives in a manner consistent with the overall risk management and capital policies approved by their boards of directors. These policies should be reviewed as business and market circumstances change. Policies governing derivatives use should be clearly defined, including the purposes for which these transactions are to be undertaken. Senior management should approve procedures and controls to implement these policies, and management at all levels should enforce them.

Derivatives activities merit senior management attention because they can generate significant benefits or costs for any firm. A firm's policies for derivatives should be an integral part of its overall policies for risk taking and management, either in its underlying business (if it is an end-user) or in its other lines of business (if it is a dealer). Periodic reviews will help ensure that these policies reflect changing circumstances and innovations.

Valuation and Market Risk Management

Recommendation 2: Marking to Market

Dealers should mark their derivatives positions to market, on at least a daily basis, for risk management purposes.

Marking to market is the only valuation technique that correctly reflects the current value of derivatives cash flows to be managed and provides information about market risk and appropriate hedging actions. Lower-of-cost-or-market accounting, and accruals accounting, are not appropriate for risk management.

The Survey of Industry Practice shows that the practice of marking to market daily is widespread among dealers, reflecting the importance of the information it provides to risk managers. Intraday or even real time valuation can help greatly, especially in managing the market risk of some option portfolios.

Recommendation 3: Market Valuation Methods

Derivatives portfolios of dealers should be valued based on mid-market levels less specific adjustments, or on appropriate bid or offer levels. Mid-market valuation adjustments should allow for expected future costs such as unearned credit spread, close-out costs, investing and funding costs, and administrative costs.

Marking to mid-market less adjustments specifically defines and quantifies adjustments that are implicitly assumed in the bid or offer method. Using the mid-market valuation method without adjustment would overstate the value of a portfolio by not deferring income to meet future costs and to provide a credit spread.

Two adjustments to mid-market are necessary even for a perfectly matched portfolio: the "unearned credit spread adjustment" to reflect the credit risk in the portfolio; and the "administrative costs adjustment" for costs that will be incurred to administer the portfolio. The unearned credit spread adjustment represents amounts set aside to cover expected credit losses and to provide compensation for credit exposure. Expected credit losses should be based upon expected exposure to counterparties (taking into account netting arrangements), expected default experience, and overall portfolio diversification. The unearned credit spread should preferably be adjusted dynamically as these factors change. It can be calculated on a transaction basis, on a portfolio basis, or across all activities with a given client.

Two additional adjustments are necessary for portfolios that are not perfectly matched: the "close-out costs adjustment" which factors in the cost of eliminating their market risk; and the "investing and funding costs adjustment" relating to the cost of funding and investing cash flow mismatches at rates different from the LIBOR rate which models typically assume.

The Survey reveals a wide range of practice concerning the mark-to-market method and the use of adjustments to mid-market value. The most commonly used adjustments are for credit and administrative costs.

Recommendation 4: Identifying Revenue Sources
Dealers should measure the components of revenue regularly and in sufficient detail to understand the sources of risk.

By identifying and isolating individual sources of revenue, dealers develop a more refined understanding of the risks and returns of derivatives activities. Components of revenue generally include origination revenue, credit spread revenue, if applicable, and other trading revenue. It is useful, though complex, to split other trading revenue among components of market risk.

The Survey of Industry Practice indicates that few dealers identify individual sources of revenue. This should become a more common practice.

Recommendation 5: Measuring Market Risk
Dealers should use a consistent measure to calculate daily the market risk of their derivatives positions and compare it to market risk limits.

- *Market risk is best measured as "value at risk" using probability analysis based upon a common confidence interval (e.g., two standard deviations) and time horizon (e.g., a one-day exposure).*

- *Components of market risk that should be considered across the term structure include: absolute price or rate change (delta); convexity (gamma); volatility (vega); time decay (theta); basis or correlation; and discount rate (rho).*

Reducing market risks across derivatives to a single common denominator makes aggregation, comparison, and risk control easier. "Value at risk" is the expected loss from an adverse market movement with a specified probability over a particular period of time. For example, with 97.5% probability (that is, a "confidence interval" of 97.5%), corresponding to calculations using about two standard deviations, it can be determined that any change in portfolio value over one day resulting from an adverse market movement will not exceed a specific amount. Conversely, there is a 2.5% probability of experiencing an adverse change in excess of the calculated amount.

Value at risk should encompass changes in all major market risk components listed in the recommendation. The difficulty in applying the technique of value at risk increases with the complexity of the risks being managed. For comparability, value at risk should be calculated to a common confidence interval and time horizon.

For most portfolios without options, once the expected loss is known for events with a given probability, the loss for a more likely or less likely scenario can easily be deduced. Therefore, for such portfolios, the choice of confidence interval is of no great significance. For option-based portfolios, however, this does not hold true. In their case, it would also be useful to calculate the loss from more and less likely scenarios.

A time horizon of one day is consistent with Recommendation 2 for daily marking to market, which allows management to know and decide daily any change of the risk profile.

Once a method of risk measurement is in place, market risk limits must be decided based on factors such as: management tolerance for low probability extreme losses versus higher probability modest losses; capital resources; market liquidity; expected profitability; trader experience; and business strategy.

The Survey suggests that most dealers know and consider some or all of the components of market risk. However, the use of one consistent measure of market risk, such as value at risk, is more prevalent among large dealers.

Recommendation 6: Stress Simulations
Dealers should regularly perform simulations to determine how their portfolios would perform under stress conditions.

Simulations of improbable market environments are important in risk analysis because many assumptions that are valid for normal markets may no longer hold true in abnormal markets.

These simulations should reflect both historical events and future possibilities. Stress scenarios should include not only abnormally large market swings but also periods of prolonged inactivity. The tests should consider the effect of price changes on the mid-market value of the portfolio, as well as changes in the assumptions about the adjustments to mid-market (such as the impact that decreased liquidity would have on close-out costs). Dealers should evaluate the results of stress tests and develop contingency plans accordingly.

The Survey indicates that some stress testing is being conducted, mainly by large dealers, and that broader usage is planned.

Recommendation 7: Investing and Funding Forecasts
Dealers should periodically forecast the cash investing and funding requirements arising from their derivatives portfolios.

The frequency and precision of forecasts should be determined by the size and nature of mismatches. A detailed forecast should determine surpluses and funding needs, by currency, over time. It also should examine the potential impact of contractual unwind provisions or other credit provisions that produce cash or collateral receipts or payments.

The Survey indicates that at present, half of responding dealers are conducting forecasts of cash investing and funding requirements. This type of forecast should become a more common practice.

Recommendation 8: Independent Market Risk Management
Dealers should have a market risk management function, with clear independence and authority, to ensure that the following responsibilities are carried out:

- *The development of risk limit policies and the monitoring of transactions and positions for adherence to these policies. (See Recommendation 5.)*

- *The design of stress scenarios to measure the impact of market conditions, however improbable, that might cause market gaps, volatility swings, or disruptions of major relationships, or might reduce liquidity in the face of unfavorable market linkages, concentrated market making, or credit exhaustion. (See Recommendation 6.)*

- *The design of revenue reports quantifying the contribution of various risk components, and of market risk measures such as value at risk. (See Recommendations 4 and 5.)*

- *The monitoring of variance between the actual volatility of portfolio value and that predicted by the measure of market risk.*

- *The review and approval of pricing models and valuation systems used by front- and back-office personnel, and the development of reconciliation procedures if different systems are used.*

The growth of activities in derivatives and other financial instruments has led many firms to establish market (and credit) risk management functions to assist senior management in establishing consistent policies and procedures applicable to various activities. Market risk management is typically headed by a board level or near board level executive.

The market risk management function acts as a catalyst for the development of sound market risk management systems, models, and procedures. Its review of trading performance typically answers the question: Are results consistent with those suggested by analysis of value at risk? The risk management function is rarely involved in actual risk-taking decisions.

According to the Survey, a large majority of dealers already have such a function in place and over 50% of those that do not, plan to establish one in the near future.

Recommendation 9: Practices by End-Users

As appropriate to the nature, size, and complexity of their derivatives activities, end-users should adopt the same valuation and market risk management practices that are recommended for dealers. Specifically, they should consider: regularly marking to market their derivatives transactions for risk management purposes; periodically forecasting the cash investing and funding requirements arising from their derivatives transactions; and establishing a clearly independent and authoritative function to design and assure adherence to prudent risk limits.

While many end-users do not expect significant change in the combined value of their derivatives positions and the underlying positions, others do. Derivatives are customer-specific transactions, often designed to offset precisely the market risk of an end-user's business position (e.g., buying a commodity as a raw material). End-users should establish the performance assessment and control procedures that are appropriate for their derivatives activities.

Less than half of those end-users surveyed currently mark their derivatives hedges to market for risk management purposes. About half plan to do so.

Credit Risk Measurement and Management

Recommendation 10: Measuring Credit Exposure

Dealers and end-users should measure credit exposure on derivatives in two ways:

- *Current exposure, which is the replacement cost of derivatives transactions, that is, their market value.*

- *Potential exposure, which is an estimate of the future replacement cost of derivatives transactions. It should be calculated using probability analysis based upon broad confidence intervals (e.g., two standard deviations) over the remaining terms of the transactions.*

To assess credit risk, a dealer or end-user should ask two questions. If a counterparty was to default today, what would it cost to replace the derivatives transaction? If a counterparty defaults in the future, what is a reasonable estimate of the future replacement cost?

Current exposure is an accurate measure of credit risk that addresses the first question. It simply evaluates the replacement cost of outstanding derivatives commitments. The result can be positive or negative. It is an important measure of credit risk as it represents the actual risk to a counterparty at any point in time. The regular calculation of current exposure is a broadly accepted practice today.

Potential exposure is more difficult to assess, and the methods used to determine it vary. The most rigorous methods use either simulation analysis or option valuation models. The analysis generally involves a statistical modeling of the effects on the value of the derivatives of movement in the prices of the underlying variables (such as interest rates, exchange rates, equity prices, or commodity prices). These techniques are often used to generate two measures of potential exposure: expected exposure; and maximum or "worst case" exposure.

Dealers and end-users that cannot justify the simulation and statistical systems needed to perform such potential exposure calculations should use tables of factors developed under the same principles. The factors used should differentiate appropriately by type and maturity of transaction and be adjusted periodically for changes in market conditions.

The Survey shows that dealers use several different methods for calculating credit exposures. These include: the BIS original and current exposure methods, used by one-third of all dealers; methods based on worst-case scenarios applied to each transaction, used by about a quarter of dealers and expected to become the most common in the future; and methods that rely upon tables of factors, used by almost 40% of dealers. End-users tend to rely on simpler methods primarily based on notional amounts.

Recommendation 11: Aggregating Credit Exposures
Credit exposures on derivatives, and all other credit exposures to a counterparty, should be aggregated taking into consideration enforceable netting arrangements. Credit exposures should be calculated regularly and compared to credit limits.

In calculating the current credit exposure for a portfolio of transactions with a counterparty, the first question is whether netting applies. If it does, the current exposure is simply the sum of positive and negative exposures on transactions in the portfolio.

The calculation of potential exposure is more complicated. Simply summing the potential exposures of all transactions will in most cases dramatically overstate the actual exposure, even if netting does not apply. This is because a straight summation fails to take into account transactions in the portfolio that offset each other or that have peak potential exposures at different times. The most accurate calculation of potential exposure simulates the entire portfolio. Although portfolio-level simulation is not commonly used by dealers at present, they should pursue it more widely to avoid overstating aggregate exposure.

Credit exposures should be calculated regularly. In particular, dealers should monitor current exposures daily; they can generally measure potential exposures less frequently. End-users with derivative portfolios should also periodically assess credit exposures. For them, the appropriate frequency will depend upon how material their credit exposures are.

Credit exposures should also be regularly compared to credit limits, and systems should be in place to monitor when limits are approached or exceeded, so that management can take appropriate actions.

By aggregating credit exposures on derivatives as described above, participants will have a consistent basis for comparison with other credit exposures including those resulting from on-balance-sheet activity. This would permit a more effective evaluation of the adequacy of credit reserves relative to overall credit exposure.

The Survey suggests that most dealers monitor gross credit use against limits. Aggregating current and potential exposures by counterparty on a net basis is not common among dealers, although some who do not net at present plan to in the future. Frequent monitoring of credit exposure is widespread among dealers, with three-quarters of respondents doing it either intraday or overnight. The majority of end-users monitor credit exposures at least once a month.

Recommendation 12: Independent Credit Risk Management

Dealers and end-users should have a credit risk management function with clear independence and authority, and with analytical capabilities in derivatives, responsible for:

- *Approving credit exposure measurement standards.*

- *Setting credit limits and monitoring their use.*

- *Reviewing credits and concentrations of credit risk.*

- *Reviewing and monitoring risk reduction arrangements.*

For dealers, credit exposures should be monitored by an independent credit risk management group. According to the Survey, most dealers and some end-users have such a group. For end-users, this role may not necessarily be performed by a separate group; however, the credit risk should be managed independently from dealing personnel. This separation of responsibility is intended to prevent conflicts of interest and to ensure that credit exposure is assessed objectively. The credit risk management function should approve exposure management standards, and should establish credit limits for counterparties consistent with these standards. Specifically, it should conduct an internal credit review before engaging in transactions with a counterparty, and should guide the use of documentation and credit support tools. Credit limits and guidelines should ensure that only those potential counterparties that meet the appropriate credit standards, with or without credit support, become actual counterparties.

The credit risk management function should continually review the creditworthiness of counterparties and their credit limits.

Recommendation 13: Master Agreements

Dealers and end-users are encouraged to use one master agreement as widely as possible with each counterparty to document existing and future derivatives transactions, including foreign exchange forwards and options. Master agreements should provide for payments netting and close-out netting, using a full two-way payments approach.

Participants should use one master agreement with each counterparty. That agreement should provide for close-out and settlement netting as widely as possible to document derivatives transactions. In particular, there is substantial scope for reducing credit risk by including foreign exchange forwards and options under master agreements along with other derivatives transactions.

A single master agreement that documents transactions between two parties creates the greatest legal certainty that credit exposure will be netted. The use of multiple master agreements between two parties introduces the risk of "cherry-picking" among master agreements (rather than among individual transactions); and the risk that the right to set off amounts due under different master agreements might be delayed. Dealers and end-users will be well served by using a single master agreement with counterparties to document as many derivatives transactions as law or regulation permit. The practices of using separate agreements for each transaction between two parties, or standard terms that do not constitute a master agreement, are not good practices and should be discontinued. According to the Survey, two-fifths of all dealers now document derivatives transactions under a multi-product master, and more plan to do so in the future.

Full two-way payments, as opposed to limited two-way payments, is now the preferred payments approach in master agreements. Under full two-way payments, the net amount calculated through the netting provisions in a bilateral master agreement is due regardless of whether it is to, or from, the defaulting party. Under limited two-way payments, the defaulting party is not entitled to receive anything, even if the net amount is in its favor. This discourages default and enhances cross-product and cross-affiliate set-off. However, when master agreements cover a wide range of derivatives transactions, the benefits created by increasing the certainty about the value of a net position under full two-way payments outweigh any possible benefits under limited two-way payments.

Recommendation 14: Credit Enhancement

Dealers and end-users should assess both the benefits and costs of credit enhancement and related risk-reduction arrangements. Where it is proposed that credit downgrades would trigger early termination or collateral requirements, participants should carefully consider their own capacity and that of their counterparties to meet the potentially substantial funding needs that might result.

Credit risk reduction arrangements can be useful in the management of counterparty credit risk. These include collateral and margin arrangements; third-party credit enhancement such as guarantees or letters of credit; and structural credit enhancement through the establishment of special-purpose vehicles to conduct derivatives business.

The Survey indicates that about two-thirds of dealers are prepared to accept credit enhancement with cash or securities as collateral, and over three-quarters accept a third party guarantee or enhancement. Reflecting strong dealer credit ratings, only one-third are prepared to provide cash or securities collateral and only 10% or so will offer a third party guarantee.

Enforceability

Recommendation 15: Promoting Enforceability

Dealers and end-users should work together on a continuing basis to identify and recommend solutions for issues of legal enforceability, both within and across jurisdictions, as activities evolve and new types of transactions are developed.

Dealers regularly develop new types of transactions, and new technologies are developed to confirm them. These developments may not fit clearly within the current legal framework in the jurisdictions where transactions occur. Therefore, dealers and end-users should continue to work together to evaluate developments in light of existing laws to assess what legal issues may arise. They should take the initiative to ensure that risks arising from these developments can be properly handled through analysis, market practices, documentation and, when necessary, legislation.

Enforceability of netting provisions is considered a serious concern by 43% of dealer senior management responding to the Survey, and another 45% consider it to be of some concern. It also is considered a serious issue by management of many end-users.

Systems, Operations, and Controls

Recommendation 16: Professional Expertise
Dealers and end-users must ensure that their derivatives activities are undertaken by professionals in sufficient number and with the appropriate experience, skill levels, and degrees of specialization. These professionals include specialists who transact and manage the risks involved, their supervisors, and those responsible for processing, reporting, controlling, and auditing the activities.

To establish good management, derivatives activities must be staffed by talented, well-trained, and responsible professionals. There is a danger, however, in relying on a few specialists, and it is essential that their managers understand not only derivatives but also the broader business context.

Derivatives support functions are technical and generally require a level of expertise higher than for other financial instruments or activities. Respondents to the Survey expressed concern that, while they are satisfied with the quality of staff in line derivatives activities, the quality of support staff lags. Developing expertise through training programs and appropriate standards of professionalism is encouraged.

The Survey indicates that, for the majority of respondent dealers, senior management is confident about the general quality of its derivatives professionals. To the extent it is concerned about issues of professionalism, it is more worried about its own lack of understanding, about insufficient understanding of derivatives by other functions, and about overreliance on a few specialists.

Recommendation 17: Systems
Dealers and end-users must ensure that adequate systems for data capture, processing, settlement, and management reporting are in place so that derivatives transactions are conducted in an orderly and efficient manner in compliance with management policies. Dealers should have risk management systems that measure the risks incurred in their derivatives activities including market and credit risks. End-users should have risk management systems that measure the risks incurred in their derivatives activities based upon their nature, size, and complexity.

The size and scope of the required systems will depend upon the nature and scale of an organization's derivatives transactions.

For dealers, operating efficiency and reliability are enhanced through the development of systems that minimize manual intervention. Those benefits are particularly significant for dealers with a large volume of activity and a high degree of customization of transactions. At the moment, confirmations of transactions, for example, are automated for about 40% of dealers, some 10% are partially automated, and another 45% rely on manual systems. Eighty percent plan to automate their confirmations completely. In addition, large dealers have made significant investments to integrate back- and front-office systems for derivatives with their firms' other management information systems. Dealers that have done so have found that the integration further enhances operating efficiency and reliability.

While end-users may invest less extensively in their systems than dealers do, these should still be sufficient to group exposures and analyze aggregated risk in a meaningful and useful way.

Recommendation 18: Authority
Management of dealers and end-users should designate who is authorized to commit their institutions to derivatives transactions.

Authority may be delegated to certain individuals or to persons holding certain positions within the firm. Management may choose to limit authority to certain types of transactions, for example to certain maturities, amounts, or types of underlying risks. It is essential that this information be understood within the firm.

Participants should communicate information on which individuals have the authority to commit to counterparties. They should recognize, however, that the legal doctrine of "apparent authority" may govern the transactions they enter into, and that there is no substitute for appropriate internal controls.

Two-thirds of dealers responding to the Survey involve senior management in authorizing traders to commit the firm.

Accounting and Disclosure

Recommendation 19: Accounting Practices
International harmonization of accounting standards for derivatives is desirable. Pending the adoption of harmonized standards, the following accounting practices are recommended:

- *Dealers should account for derivatives transactions by marking them to market, taking changes in value to income each period.*

- *End-users should account for derivatives used to manage risks so as to achieve a consistency of income recognition treatment between those instruments and the risks being managed. Thus, if the risk being managed is accounted for at cost (or, in the case of an anticipatory hedge, not yet recognized), changes in the value of a qualifying risk management instrument should be deferred until a gain or loss is recognized on the risk being managed. Or, if the risk being managed is marked to market with changes in value being taken to income, a qualifying risk management instrument should be treated in a comparable fashion.*

- *End-users should account for derivatives not qualifying for risk management treatment on a mark-to-market basis.*

* *Amounts due to and from counterparties should only be offset when there is a legal right to set off or when enforceable netting arrangements are in place.*

Where local regulations prevent adoption of these practices, disclosure along these lines is nevertheless recommended.

Accounting policies for derivatives vary widely around the world. In some countries there are local accounting standards that address accounting for derivatives; in other countries there are no specific standards and a variety of customs and practices has developed. In view of the global nature of derivatives, it is desirable to achieve some harmonization of accounting treatment to assist in clarifying the financial statements of dealers and end-users.

The recommendation for dealers to account for changes in the value of their derivatives positions in income during each period has become standard in many, although not all, countries. It provides a better representation of the economic effects of such positions than other methods.

The recommended accounting treatment for end-users using derivatives to manage risks, referred to as "risk management accounting," is also a standard treatment. It has evolved in many countries, at least in a modified form, as a response to anomalies in the existing accounting framework. Traditionally in some countries, this accounting treatment has been applied solely to transactions undertaken to reduce risks, usually referred to as "hedges."

Policies must define when financial instruments are eligible for risk management accounting to ensure that the method is not abused.

Among a majority of dealers who responded to the Survey, senior management thought inconsistency of accounting standards with the economics of the business were either of serious or some concern.

Recommendation 20: Disclosures

Financial statements of dealers and end-users should contain sufficient information about their use of derivatives to provide an understanding of the purposes for which transactions are undertaken, the extent of the transactions, the degree of risk involved, and how the transactions have been accounted for. Pending the adoption of harmonized accounting standards, the following disclosures are recommended:

- *Information about management's attitude to financial risks, how instruments are used, and how risks are monitored and controlled.*

- *Accounting policies.*

- *Analysis of positions at the balance sheet date.*

- *Analysis of the credit risk inherent in those positions.*

- *For dealers only, additional information about the extent of their activities in financial instruments.*

The Survey shows that the quality of financial statement disclosure about derivatives transactions varies even more widely than the accounting policies that are applied. Until local standards-setting bodies can adopt harmonized standards, there is a need to improve the quality of financial statement disclosure concerning transactions in both derivatives and cash market instruments.

Its qualitative nature dictates that information about management's attitude to financial risks, how instruments are used, and how risks are monitored and controlled, should appear in the management analysis section of the annual report. The remaining information should appear in the footnotes to the financial statements and be commented on as appropriate in the management analysis.

This recommendation is not apparently precluded by accounting regulations in any country and its early adoption is encouraged.

Inadequate public disclosure of exposures of counterparties is of some concern, or of serious concern, to about three-fifths of senior management among dealers responding to the Survey.

Recommendations for Legislators, Regulators, and Supervisors

Recommendation 21: Recognizing Netting

Regulators and supervisors should recognize the benefits of netting arrangements where and to the full extent that they are enforceable, and encourage their use by reflecting these arrangements in capital adequacy standards. Specifically, they should promptly implement the recognition of the effectiveness of bilateral close-out netting in bank capital regulations.

The bilateral or multilateral netting of contractual payments due on settlement dates, and of unrealized losses against unrealized gains in the event of a counterparty's default, is the most important means of mitigating credit risk. By reducing settlement risk as well as credit exposures, netting contributes to the reduction of systemic risk.

Significant efforts have been made to develop standard master agreements that effect netting across the full range of derivatives products. Nonetheless, the enforceability of such netting provisions remains among the highest concerns of senior management of derivatives dealers, according to the Survey.

Regulators and supervisors should officially recognize netting where and to the full extent it is enforceable, and reflect these arrangements in the capital standards. In this way, regulators and supervisors will stimulate efforts to resolve uncertainties where they exist and will create tangible incentives for using this most important method of reducing counterparty risk.

An important step in implementing this recommendation was taken in April of this year when the Basle Committee released a Consultative Paper that included a proposal for recognizing the effectiveness of close-out netting. This is an amendment to the agreed framework for measuring bank capital adequacy (the "Basle Accord") published by the Basle Committee in July 1988. When the consultation period for this proposal has ended, the national supervisory authorities represented on the Basle Committee should recognize and implement bilateral close-out netting for capital purposes.

Recommendation 22: Legal and Regulatory Uncertainties

Legislators, regulators, and supervisors, including central banks, should work in concert with dealers and end-users to identify and remove any remaining legal and regulatory uncertainties with respect to:

- *The form of documentation required to create legally enforceable agreements (statute of frauds).*

- *The capacity of parties, such as governmental entities, insurance companies, pension funds, and building societies, to enter into transactions* (ultra vires).

- *The enforceability of bilateral close-out netting and collateral arrangements in bankruptcy.*

- *The enforceability of multibranch netting arrangements in bankruptcy.*

- *The legality/enforceability of derivatives transactions.*

These five main enforceability risks are analyzed for nine major jurisdictions in Appendix II (bound separately). Regulators and legislators in these jurisdictions should remove the remaining uncertainties that have been identified. In other countries, market participants, regulators, and legislators should work to identify and resolve any similar legal risks. These efforts should be conducted on a continuing basis, to account for new types of derivatives transactions and new technologies. It is important to approach these issues aggressively so that the largest risks faced by dealers and end-users are not legal risks from legal systems that have not kept pace with financial developments.

Further work on the enforceability in bankruptcy or insolvency of bilateral netting and collateral arrangements is particularly important if the credit risk reduction techniques for derivatives are to evolve. These techniques are essential building blocks for enforceable multilateral netting arrangements, if that is a direction participants choose to take.

Recommendation 23: Tax Treatment

Legislators and tax authorities are encouraged to review and, where appropriate, amend tax laws and regulations that disadvantage the use of derivatives in risk management strategies. Tax impediments include the inconsistent or uncertain tax treatment of gains and losses on the derivatives, in comparison with the gains and losses that arise from the risks being managed.

In most, if not all jurisdictions, the tax treatment being applied to derivatives transactions dates back to before they came into general use. This can lead to considerable uncertainty in determining how gains and losses associated with these instruments should be taxed depending upon their use.

These uncertainties and inconsistencies present real difficulties to organizations that seek to use derivatives to manage risks in their businesses. Confusion can discourage them from pursuing commercially sensible risk management strategies.

Recommendation 24: Accounting Standards

Accounting standards-setting bodies in each country should, as a matter of priority, provide comprehensive guidance on accounting and reporting of transactions in financial instruments, including derivatives, and should work towards international harmonization of standards on this subject. Also, the International Accounting Standards Committee should finalize its accounting standard on Financial Instruments.

At present no country has accounting and reporting standards that comprehensively address all financial instruments, including derivatives. Even in those countries where development of accounting standards is considered far advanced, there are gaps or inconsistencies between different standards. This is an area where action needs to be taken as a matter of priority.

In a number of countries, accounting standards-setters have recognized the need to improve accounting standards in this area and some have commenced work. Furthermore, the International Accounting Standards Committee (IASC) has issued an exposure draft on Financial Instruments (E40) and presently intends to finalize an accounting standard by the end of 1993.

In addressing the accounting and disclosure requirements for financial instruments, the IASC and national accounting standards-setters are encouraged to address the problems of accounting for risk management activities. Most existing accounting regulations were formulated before recent advances in risk management strategies. This poses considerable practical problems, both to end-users and dealers. Developments in accounting regulations have not kept pace with changes in the way risk is managed.

In some countries, the accounting standards that govern the eligibility for hedge accounting treatment of hedges of anticipated transactions may be too restrictive: some relaxation should be permitted, subject to safeguards to prevent abuse.

Similarly, accounting standards should deal with risk management in a broad sense and not deal just with risk reduction (hedging) which is only one aspect of risk management. Risk management strategies are increasingly being used by both financial and nonfinancial institutions to achieve an acceptable risk profile, but not necessarily a reduced level of risk. Concern over current accounting regulations is deterring some organizations from pursuing commercially sensible risk management strategies. While standards are necessary to ensure that risk management accounting is not abused, it is essential that accounting standards respond to modern risk management techniques.

Overview of Derivatives Activity

Overview of Derivatives Activity
Contents

Overview of Derivatives Activity

The creation and widespread use of global derivatives in the past 15 years have changed the face of finance. Derivatives have not only increased the range of financial products available; they have also fostered more precise ways of understanding, quantifying, and managing financial risk. Today, most major institutional borrowers and investors use derivatives. Many also act as intermediaries dealing in these transactions.

While the concept underpinning derivatives is simple, it is also flexible and powerful: a party exposed to an unwanted risk can pass that risk to another party and assume a different risk, or pay cash, in return. For example, in a swap transaction, two parties with reciprocal risks can reduce or eliminate them by exchanging payment streams. A borrower can, in effect, exchange payments on a debt in Swiss francs for an obligation in U.S. dollars. An investor can exchange the return on a basket of U.S. stocks for the return on a basket of German stocks. A purchaser of petroleum can, in effect, fix the price of future purchases in Japanese yen, Deutsche marks, or many other currencies.

The development of derivatives has occurred in response to a search for higher yields and lower funding costs and a demand for tools to manage risk. The broad demand for derivatives arises from the diverse and changing financial needs of a wide array of users, some hedging current or future risks, some taking market risk positions, and some exploiting inefficiencies between markets.

While much of the discussion that follows also applies to futures and to some securities, the focus of this Study is those derivatives that are privately negotiated contracts, offered internationally by dealers directly to end-users – so-called global or over-the-counter (OTC) derivatives. As awareness has grown that OTC derivatives have become a mainstream financial activity, they have come under scrutiny. Some observers have raised issues of good management practice and appropriate public policy.

This Overview of Derivatives Activity first defines derivatives in general and describes the use of derivatives. Next, it discusses the major types of risks that users of these derivatives must manage – market, credit, operational, and legal risks. Then, it describes the growth in global derivatives activity in the context of related markets. Finally, it addresses the impact of global derivatives on systemic risk and the overall economy.

I. What Are Derivatives?

Definition

In the most general terms, a derivatives transaction is a bilateral contract or payments exchange agreement whose value derives, as its name implies, from the value of an underlying asset or underlying reference rate or index. Today, derivatives transactions cover a broad range of "underlyings" – interest rates, exchange rates, commodities, equities, and other indices.

In addition to privately negotiated, global transactions, derivatives also include standardized futures and options on futures that are actively traded on organized exchanges, and securities such as call warrants. The term "derivative" also is used by some observers to refer to a wide variety of debt instruments that have payoff characteristics reflecting embedded derivatives, or have option characteristics, or are created by "stripping" particular components of other instruments such as principal or interest payments.

Table 1
Derivatives Contracts and Derivative Securities
Note: The Derivatives Contracts indicated in green are the primary subject of this study.

Derivatives Contracts

Privately Negotiated (OTC) Forwards	*Privately Negotiated (OTC) Options*	*Exchange Traded Futures*	*Exchange Traded Options*
Forward Commodity Contracts	Commodity Options	Eurodollar (CME)	S&P Futures Options (Merc)
Forward Foreign Exchange Contracts	Currency Options	US Treasury Bond (CBT)	Bond Futures Options (LIFFE)
	Equity Options	9% British Gilt (LIFFE)	
Forward Rate Agreements (FRAs)	FRA Options	CAC-40 (MATIF)	Corn Futures Options (CBT)
Currency Swaps	Caps, Floors, Collars	DM/$ (IMM)	Yen/$ Futures Options (IMM)
Interest Rate Swaps	Swap Options	German Bund (DTB)	
	Bond Options	Gold (COMEX)	
Commodity Swaps			
Equity Swaps			

Derivative Securities

Structured Securities and Deposits	*Stripped Securities*	*Securities with Option Characteristics*
Dual Currency Bonds	Treasury Strips	Callable Bonds
Commodity-Linked Bonds	IO's and PO's	Putable Bonds
Yield Curve Notes		Convertible Securities
Equity-Linked Bank Deposits		Warrants

The array of derivatives contracts is not as complex as it first appears. Every derivatives transaction can be built up from two simple and fundamental types of building blocks: forwards and options. Forward-based transactions include forwards and swap contracts, as well as exchange-traded futures. Option-based transactions include privately negotiated, OTC options (including caps, floors, collars, and options on forward and swap contracts) and exchange-traded options on futures. Diverse types of derivatives are created by combining the building blocks in different ways, and by applying these structures to a wide range of underlying assets, rates, or indices.

The rest of this section describes the main types of derivatives contracts.

Forward-Based Derivatives

Forward Contracts The simplest derivative is the forward contract. A forward contract obligates one counterparty to buy, and the other to sell, a specific underlying at a specific price, amount, and date in the future. Forward markets exist for a multitude of underlyings, including the traditional agricultural or physical commodities, as well as currencies (referred to as foreign exchange forwards) and interest rates (referred to as forward rate agreements or "FRAs").[1] The change in the value of a forward contract is roughly proportional to the change in the value of its underlying. This distinguishes forward-based derivatives from option-based derivatives, which have a different payoff profile (see the section on them below).

Forward contracts are customized with terms and conditions tailored to fit the particular business, financial, or risk management objectives of the counterparties. Negotiations often take place with respect to contract size, delivery grade, delivery locations, delivery dates, and credit terms. Forwards, in other words, are not standardized.

Figure 1
Value of a Forward Contract

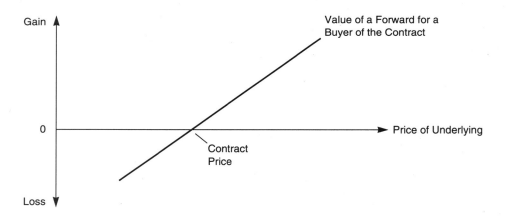

The value of a forward contract is conveyed at contract maturity through delivery or cash settlement. If, at maturity, the price of the underlying is higher than the contract price, then the buyer makes a profit. If the price is lower, the buyer suffers a loss. The gain to the buyer equals the loss to the seller. This graph describes the payoff, or the market risk, associated with a forward contract.

---

[1]The volume of activity in forward contracts is very large. Global *daily* turnover in forward transactions in the foreign exchange market is estimated at $420 billion. See "The Central Bank Survey of Foreign Exchange Market Activity in April 1992," Bank for International Settlements, March 11, 1993, Table I, page 6.

Forward contracts create credit exposures. Since the value of the contract is conveyed only at maturity, the parties are exposed to the risk of default during the life of the contract. The credit risk is two-sided. Only the party for whom the contract has a positive mark-to-market value can suffer a loss; but, since either party can ultimately end up in this situation, each party must evaluate the creditworthiness of its counterparty.

Since these contracts are typically large and the potential credit risk may be significant, the counterparties to forward contracts are usually corporations, financial institutions, institutional investors, or governmental entities.

Swap Transactions As the name implies, a swap transaction obligates the two parties to the contract to exchange a series of cash flows at specified intervals known as payment or settlement dates. The cash flows of a swap are either fixed, or calculated for each settlement date by multiplying the quantity of the underlying (notional principal) by specified reference rates or prices. Depending upon the type of underlying, the great majority of these transactions are classified into interest rate, currency, commodity, or equity swaps.[2] Except for currency swaps, the notional principal is used to calculate the payment stream but not exchanged. Interim payments are generally netted, with the difference being paid by one party to the other.

Swaps, like forwards, are bilateral agreements between sophisticated, institutional participants; they are entered into through private negotiations and give rise to credit exposures. Swaps are tailored, like forwards, to meet the specific risk management needs of the counterparties.

The cash flows from a swap can be decomposed into equivalent cash flows from a bundle of simpler forward contracts.[3] Interest rate and currency swaps can also be analyzed in economic terms as back-to-back or parallel loans.[4] Both of these decompositions have important implications for pricing and hedging. They imply pricing relationships and related arbitrage opportunities among swaps, forwards, and futures contracts and between derivatives in general and various cash market instruments. They also suggest the many ways in which the market risk of swaps can be hedged. For example, combinations of long and short positions in government or corporate securities, exchange-traded interest rate futures, or forward rate agreements can be used to hedge swap exposure – and vice versa.

---

[2] At year-end 1991, the total notional principal outstanding of interest rate and currency swaps was $3,872 billion, based on data provided by the International Swaps and Derivatives Association (ISDA).

[3] For example, an interest rate swap can be decomposed in terms of cash flows into a portfolio of single payment forward contracts on interest rates. At each settlement date, the loss or gain in the currently maturing implicit forward contract is in effect realized.

[4] For example, for the fixed-rate payor in an interest rate swap, the net cash flow is analogous to borrowing at a fixed rate and simultaneously lending at a floating rate. Since a forward rate agreement can be viewed, in terms of cash flows, as a pair of single-period fixed- and floating-rate notes, this analogy should not be surprising in light of the relationship between a swap and a bundle of forward rate agreements.

Futures Contracts The basic form of a futures contract is similar to that of a forward contract: a futures contract obligates its owner to buy a specified underlying at a specified price on the contract maturity date (or settle the value for cash). The payoff, or market risk, profile facing the owner of a futures contract is also similar to that of a forward contract. The volume of the newer financial futures contracts involving interest rates, currencies, and equity indices now dwarfs the volume in traditional agricultural contracts.[5]

Despite the similarity in payoff profiles, important economic differences distinguish futures from forwards and swaps. First, the contract terms of futures describing the quantity and quality of the underlying, the time and place of delivery, and the method of payment are fully standardized. Price is the only variable left to be determined. This standardization extends to the credit risk of futures. Credit risk is greatly reduced by marking the contract to market with daily (or more frequent) settling up of changes in value, and by requiring buyers and sellers alike to post margin as collateral for these settlement payments. This full standardization leads to fungibility – that is, contracts of the same maturity are perfect substitutes. These characteristics are designed to facilitate anonymous trading in an active and liquid exchange market.

Second, futures differ from forwards and swaps in that contractual obligations under futures contracts are entered into directly with the exchange clearinghouse and are generally satisfied through offset – the cancellation of an existing futures position through the acquisition of an equal but opposite position that leaves the clearinghouse with zero net exposure. The right to offset allows futures participants to readily cut their losses or take their profits, without negotiating with counterparties.

Finally, the anonymous nature of futures trading and the relatively small contract size make futures contracts accessible to members of the general public, including retail speculators, who are unable to transact in forwards and swaps.

Option-Based Derivatives

Option Transactions The other derivatives building block is the option contract. In exchange for payment of a premium, an option contract gives the option holder the right *but not the obligation* to buy or sell the underlying (or settle the value for cash) at a price, called the strike price, during a period or on a specific date. Thus, the owner of the option can choose not to exercise the option and let it expire. The buyer benefits from favorable movements in the price of the underlying but is not exposed to corresponding losses.

---

[5] At year-end 1991, on a worldwide basis, the total face value of the open interest in interest rate and currency futures was $2.18 trillion. The total face value of the open positions in financial futures contracts in the United States was $1.17 trillion for short-term interest rate futures contracts; $54 billion for long-term interest rate contracts; $17 billion for currency futures; and $31 billion for stock index futures contracts. Banks combined held 57% of the long and 51% of the short open positions in short-term interest rate futures. See "Recent Developments in International Interbank Relations," Bank for International Settlements, October 1992, Table 6 and Table 13.

Privately negotiated options exist on a multitude of underlyings, such as bonds, equities, currencies and commodities, and even swaps. Options also can be structured as securities such as warrants or can be embedded in securities such as certain commodity or equity-linked bonds with option-like characteristics.

Figure 2
Value of an Option Contract

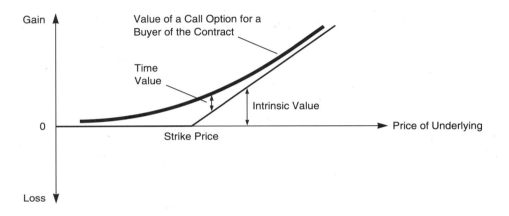

The value of an option contract (heavily shaded line) is composed of its "intrinsic" value – the payoff on the option at expiration – plus its "time" value – the value attributable to the volatility in the underlying over the remaining life of the option. The "hockey stick" profile shown by the other line reflects the intrinsic value of the option. The curved line represents the value of the option at some time prior to expiration.

Caps, Floors, and Collars Much as forwards can be bundled to create swaps, options can be bundled to create other option-based contracts called caps, floors, and collars. Like interest rate swaps, caps, floors, and collars are generally medium- to long-term transactions. A notional principal is used to calculate periodic cash flows. The buyer of the cap pays a premium, normally at inception. At each payment date, the seller must pay the buyer an amount based on the difference, if positive, between the reference and strike rate (cap). A cap therefore protects a floating-rate borrower against a rise in interest rates. A floor contract is the opposite of a cap in that payment is made only if the difference is negative. A floor therefore protects a floating-rate investor against a decline in interest rates. Buying a collar is equivalent to buying a cap and selling a floor.

Swaptions A swaption (or swap option) is an option on a swap.[6] It gives the buyer the right, but not the obligation, to enter into a specified swap contract at a future date. In this case, the asset underlying the option contract is another derivatives transaction (i.e., a swap). A borrower can buy protection against the effect of a

---

[6] An additional example of a derivative in which the underlying is another derivative contract is an option on a cap.

general rise in interest rates through the purchase of an option to enter into an interest rate swap. Swaptions now play an important role in the management of corporate debt, especially callable debt.[7]

Options on Futures Contracts Options on futures contracts are to OTC options what futures contracts are to forward contracts and swaps. They have similar payoff profiles but differ from OTC options in that they are fully standardized (including credit terms), can be cancelled through offset, and can be traded by the general public.[8]

II. Who Uses Derivatives and Why?

The participants in derivatives activity can be divided into two groups – end-users and dealers. End-users consist of corporations, governmental entities, institutional investors, and financial institutions. Dealers consist mainly of banks and securities firms, with a few insurance companies and highly rated corporations (mainly energy firms) having recently joined the ranks. An institution may participate in derivatives activity both as an end-user and a dealer. For example, a money-center bank acts as an end-user when it uses derivatives to take positions as part of its proprietary trading or for hedging as part of its asset and liability management. It acts as a dealer when it quotes bids and offers and commits capital to satisfying customers' demands for derivatives.

Derivatives permit end-users and dealers to identify, isolate, and manage separately the fundamental risks and other characteristics that are bound together in traditional financial instruments. Desired combinations of cash flow, interest rate, currency, liquidity, and market source characteristics can be achieved largely by separable choices, each independent of the underlying cash market instrument. As a result, management is able to think and act in terms of fundamental risks.

The next section describes specific uses of derivatives by different groups of end-users.

End-Users
Derivatives are used by end-users to lower funding costs, enhance yields, diversify sources of funding, hedge, and express market views through position taking.

Corporations According to the Survey of Industry Practice, over 80% of the private sector corporations consider derivatives either very important (44%) or imperative (37%) for controlling risk. Roughly 87% of the reporting private sector corporations

---

[7] At year-end 1991, the total notional principal outstanding of caps, collars, floors, and swaptions in all currencies was $577 billion based on data provided by ISDA.

[8] At year-end 1991, the total face value of open positions in options on futures contracts (calls plus puts) in the United States was $628 billion for short-term interest rates and $32 billion for currencies. Banks held over 45% of the open call positions and over 42% of the put positions on short-term interest rates futures contracts. See "Recent Developments in International Interbank Relations," Bank for International Settlements, October 1992, Table 14, page 57.

use interest rate swaps, while 64% use currency swaps and 78% use forward foreign exchange contracts. For option-based derivatives, 40% use interest rate options and 31% use currency options.

Different uses of derivatives by corporations are discussed in more detail below.

Lowering Funding Costs through Arbitrage Opportunities or Issuance of Customized Instruments Derivatives allow corporations to lower funding costs by taking advantage of differences that exist between capital markets. They allow the principle of comparative advantage to be applied to financing. Where financial markets are segmented nationally or internationally, whether due to market or regulatory barriers or to different perceptions of credit qualities in various markets, the use of derivatives has delivered unambiguous cost savings for borrowers and higher yields for investors.

For example, a borrower may issue debt where it has a comparative advantage, and use a currency swap to achieve funding in its desired currency at a lower funding cost than a direct financing. A borrower generating savings in this way is, in effect, using a swap to exploit an arbitrage between the financial markets involved. Similarly, borrowers are able to achieve savings by issuing structured securities tailored to meet specific investor requirements. Then, the borrowers use swaps to achieve the borrowing currency and structure they need.[9]

The Connection Between Swaps and Financing: *In light of the significant reductions in funding costs that swap arbitrage can achieve, evaluating swap opportunities has become a crucial consideration in issuing bonds. That is, the choice of market and timing of issuance is driven by relative swap opportunities. It has been estimated that from 1985 to 1989, the volume of international new issues that were swap driven increased steadily, reaching 70% of international U.S. dollar new issue volume and 53% of total international new issue volume. Today all major borrowers monitor their funding opportunities regularly by evaluating the relative pricings for new issues and swaps across markets worldwide. See* Global Swap Markets *(IFR Publishing, 1991), Table 3.*

Diversifying Funding Sources By obtaining financing from one market and then swapping all or part of the cash flows into the desired currency denominations and rate indices, issuers can diversify their funding activities across global markets. Placing debt with new investors may increase liquidity and reduce funding costs for the issuer.

Funding Operations in Multiple Countries at Lowest Cost For international corporations, borrowing needs in a particular country or countries may be too small to be funded cost effectively through the local capital markets. It may be cost effective, however, to borrow more than they need in those capital markets and swap excess debt into the other needed currencies.

---

[9] In the early days of the swap market, funding could be obtained at savings of as much as 50 basis points (0.50%) given the significant arbitrage opportunities that then were available. Today arbitrage savings are more likely to be in the range of 10 to 25 basis points (0.10% to 0.25%).

Hedging the Cost of Anticipated Issuance of Fixed-Rate Debt Volatile interest rates create uncertainty about the future cost of issuing fixed-rate debt. Delayed start swaps, or forward swaps, can be used to "lock in" the general level of interest rates that exists at the time the funding decision is made. Such hedging eliminates general market risk. It does not eliminate, however, specific risk – the risk that an issuer's funding cost may move out of line with the funding cost of other borrowers, due to factors related principally to the issuer.

Hedging the Cost of Issuing Floating-Rate Debt Issuing floating-rate debt exposes the issuer to the risk of interest rate increases over the life of the liability. A floating-rate borrower can limit his risk by purchasing a cap.[10] A borrower can also limit the fluctuation of a floating-rate borrowing by purchasing a collar. Alternatively put, the cost of the cap can be offset by selling a floor (i.e., giving up some of the gain from falling interest rates) to create a collar.

Hedging Interest Rate Risk with Caps and Collars: *Ocean Spray, makers of cranberry-based products, and Muzak, a provider of office music, managed their interest rate risks with caps and collars. Ocean Spray has a large seasonal cash requirement which it meets with floating-rate borrowings. To protect itself against sharply higher short-term rates, it used interest rate caps. The company chose to use caps rather than interest rate swaps or collars because it viewed the hedge as insurance against large, unfavorable rate changes and wanted to be able to take advantage of falling rates. Muzak, on the other hand, used a two-year collar when it recently refinanced some floating-rate debt. Muzak was looking for insurance against sharply higher rates; but to reduce the cost of the interest rate cap, Muzak sold a floor at the same time. See* Corporate Cashflow, *March and May 1990.*

Over 82% of the private sector corporations responding to the Survey indicate that they use derivatives to hedge the market risks arising from new financings.

Managing Existing Debt or Asset Portfolios As its assessment of economic prospects changes, a company may want to change the characteristics of its existing debt portfolio – either the mix of fixed- and floating-rate debt or the mix of currency denominations. Interest rate swaps can be used to adjust the ratio of fixed- to floating-rate debt, while currency swaps can be used to transform an obligation in one currency into an obligation in another currency, changing the currency mix of the debt portfolio.

---

[10] A fixed-rate borrower, on the other hand, can benefit from lower rates by purchasing a floor.

Making Small Business Loans and Adding Lending Capacity Using Interest Rate Swaps: *Two of the primary lenders to McDonald's U.S. franchisees use swaps to better accommodate franchisees' needs for financing. One of these lenders had accumulated a large portfolio of fixed-rate loans to the franchisees. It sold participations in these loans in the secondary market to investors who were willing to buy a portion of the portfolio if they could receive a floating-rate return. Interest rate swaps were used to convert the fixed-interest payment stream on the participations to the floating rate that investors desired. This freed lending capacity so the bank could make additional loans to franchisees. Another lender manages a special purpose corporation which issues commercial paper to fund franchisee loans. It uses interest rate swaps to offer McDonald's franchisees either floating- or fixed-rate funding.*

Volatile interest rates may affect the value of a firm's assets as well as its liabilities. To protect the firm's net worth from interest rate risk, corporate treasurers increasingly take account of the interest rate sensitivity of both assets and liabilities in designing hedges. Interest rate swaps can be used to adjust the average maturity or interest rate sensitivity of a company's debt portfolio so that it more closely matches the interest rate sensitivity of the asset side of the balance sheet, reducing the exposure of the company's net worth or market value to interest rate risk.

Roughly 78% of the private sector corporations responding to the Survey indicate that they use derivatives to manage or modify the characteristics of their existing liabilities and assets.

Managing Foreign Exchange Exposures Both importers and exporters are exposed to exchange rate risk. As a result of this transactional exposure, an importer's profit margin can, and often does, evaporate if its domestic currency weakens sharply before purchases have been paid for. International firms with overseas operations also face translation exposure as the values of their overseas assets and liabilities are translated into domestic currency for accounting purposes. The competitive position of many domestic producers also is subject to change with major movements in foreign exchange rates. Currency swaps and foreign exchange forwards and options can be used to create hedges of those future cash flows and reduce the risk from currency fluctuations.

Hedging Currency Risk with Forwards, Options, and Swaps: *The Intel corporation actively hedged transaction exposures arising out of its European operations in the mid-1980s. With few local currency expenses, Intel had no natural hedge against fluctuations in the value of sales made outside the United States. The problem was the relatively long times between Intel's price commitment, invoicing, and subsequent receipt of funds. Intel hedged approximately 90% of its order backlog using options to ensure that it was not left with a currency position in the event orders were cancelled. Once booked, however, the position was hedged 100% in the forward market. The company aggregated its exposure and hedged on a net basis through an operation in London. Positions were monitored closely and the size of hedges was adjusted monthly as necessary. See* Corporate Finance, *September 1987.*

Among Survey respondents, 69% of the private sector corporations report hedging foreign exchange transaction exposures while over 33% hedge translation exposures.

Managing Commodity Price Exposures Volatility in commodity prices, such as oil or copper, creates significant risk exposures for producers or firms using these or closely related commodities as inputs. These exposures can be hedged using commodity forwards, swaps, caps, or collars.

Derivatives are currently used to manage energy or raw materials costs by 11% of companies responding to the Survey.

Governmental Entities Governmental entities, including national governments, local governments, state-owned or sponsored entities, and supranationals use derivatives for much the same reasons as non-financial corporations. They use derivatives in financing activities to diversify their sources of funds and achieve cost savings through arbitrage of international and national capital markets and issuance of hedged structured securities. Derivatives are also used for debt management purposes, especially by those governments borrowing in many different currencies.

Managing Sovereign Debt with Currency Swaps: *Finland is a highly rated sovereign and an active borrower in the international capital markets. The government of Finland, through the Ministry of Finance, has actively used swaps to lower its effective cost of debt and manage the currency composition of its foreign liabilities to hedge foreign exchange risks. During the period 1987-1990, Finland entered into approximately 50 swaps with notional principal equivalent to U.S. $50-200 million at a time. Roughly 30% of the government's total outstanding foreign debt was swapped, with most swaps being related to newly issued debt. Swaps were used in 1990 to achieve funding costs of 30-50 basis points below LIBOR. They were also used to configure the currency composition of Finland's foreign liabilities in the direction of its official currency basket. The Finnish mark was pegged to the value of the currency basket. The Ministry used currency swaps to access the lowest-cost offshore debt markets, while translating the currency composition of the debt portfolio to the desired mix. Substantial changes in the debt composition were achieved through swaps. For example, although the actual share of the Japanese yen in the external debt was 23% in 1989, currency swaps were used to reduce the effective share to 12% in 1989 and 5% in 1990. See "Government Use of Cross Currency Swaps" in* Cross Currency Swaps *(Business One Irwin, 1992) edited by Carl Beidleman.*

The use of swaps by supranational entities such as The World Bank is longstanding, dating back to the first large-scale, widely publicized currency swap transaction in 1981 between IBM and The World Bank. At the federal level in the United States, government-sponsored enterprises such as the Federal National Mortgage Association and the Student Loan Marketing Association are significant users of the derivatives markets for risk management and as hedges related to structured financings.

Recently, some governmental entities have turned to commodity derivatives to manage oil price risk.

Hedging Fuel Costs with Commodity Swaps and Caps: *By mid 1991, numerous governments and municipal authorities, including Atlanta, Boston, San Francisco, Washington, DC, and Delaware, were using derivatives to lock in or cap fuel costs as a way of controlling their energy budgets. For example, the Metropolitan Atlanta Rapid Transit Authority (MARTA) entered into a one-year commodity swap in May 1991 to lock in a fuel price for its budget. The swap contract guaranteed MARTA a price of 53.3¢ per gallon for No. 2 heating oil on nine million gallons of fuel purchased during the 1991-1992 fiscal year. The transaction is estimated to have saved MARTA more than $1.5 million over actual market prices. The state of Delaware, on the other hand, chose to use heating oil price caps to control the maximum per gallon cost of fuel for its fiscal year 1992 budget. The state bought caps on 6 million gallons of No. 2 oil and No. 4 oil and 600,000 gallons of No. 6 oil for an up-front premium of $150,000 or slightly more than 2¢ per gallon. See* Corporate Risk Management, *June 1991 and September 1991.*

Institutional Investors

Enhancing Yields Through Arbitrage Opportunities The earliest use of swaps by institutional investors involved asset swaps, in which the cash flows from a particular asset are swapped for other cash flows, possibly denominated in another currency or based on a different interest rate. Institutional investors use derivatives to create investments with a higher yield than corresponding traditional investments. They might do this when securities trade poorly because of some unattractive feature. In such a case, an investor may purchase the securities, neutralize the undesirable feature with a suitable derivatives transaction, and create, for example, a synthetic fixed-rate investment with a higher yield than comparable fixed-rate instruments of the same credit quality.

Managing Exposures to Alternative Assets Institutional investors have recently begun to use derivatives, especially interest rate and equity swaps, to manage their exposure to debt and equity markets, both domestic and international. The immediate appeal is the ability to quickly and effectively adjust exposures – between debt and equity or among different equity classes – without incurring substantial transaction and custodial costs. There is also potential to enhance yields. The availability of equity swaps on the major international equity indices allows investors to diversify globally and adjust their portfolios in a cost-effective manner.

Eliminating Currency Risk Some institutional investors wish to benefit from investment in or exposure to foreign debt or equity markets without necessarily incurring foreign exchange risk. For instance, a Japanese investor might want to earn a return based on the S&P 500 Index but payable in yen at a predetermined exchange rate. A family of swaps called "quanto" swaps have been designed to meet the growing demands of investors for investment diversification without currency risk.

Managing Risk Exposures with Customized Instruments Institutional investors have benefitted from the creation of customized structured securities in which the principal redemption, coupons, or both are indexed to an underlying. These structured securities are equivalent to combinations of derivatives and traditional credit extension instruments, such as bonds, loans, or deposits. They meet the particular investment needs of the institutional investors and allow corporations to raise funds at a lower all-in cost. Corporations, banks, and government borrowers that issue these instruments typically use derivatives to hedge the unwanted risk and create attractively priced synthetic fixed- or floating-rate liabilities in the currency of their choice.

Structured Securities: *Structured securities have been around for a long time and take many forms. The nature and advantages of these products can be illustrated with examples of notes offered by Sohio, Sallie Mae, and General Electric Capital Corporation.*

Notes with the principal redemption indexed to the price of oil were offered by Sohio in June 1986. The notes maturing in 1990 paid a principal amount of $1,000 plus "the excess of the Crude Oil Price ... over $25 multiplied by 170 barrels of Light Sweet Crude Oil." The maximum indexed payment was capped at $15 per barrel. This hybrid debt, in terms of cash flows, was equivalent to a zero-coupon note coupled with a capped call option on oil.

In February 1986, Sallie Mae issued reverse floating rate notes, called "Yield Curve Notes," which paid a coupon equal to 17.2% minus LIBOR. As LIBOR fell, the coupon on the issue rose. This structured security is equivalent to a fixed-rate note combined with a swap (i.e., receive fixed – pay floating) having a notional principal equal to the principal of the loan.

In May of 1993, General Electric Capital Corporation issued $59 million of 5-year medium-term notes, called "Dollarized Yield Curve Notes," which paid semiannual coupons in U.S. dollars of 17.55% minus 75% of the sum of 6-month Lira LIBOR and 6-month Swedish Krona interbank rate. This is a multicurrency security with "quanto" features. A United States purchaser of the note obtained exposure to Italian and Swedish interest rates without being exposed to foreign exchange risk.

Many structured securities exhibit risk/return characteristics similar to global derivatives. Most are sold to sophisticated institutional investors capable of analyzing their risk/return, leverage, and liquidity characteristics. Institutional investors typically operate within a set of investment guidelines, with regulatory supervision for some. It is important, however, that institutional investors understand and manage the risks of the securities they are purchasing. The risk management aspects of structured securities are largely similar to those that underlie derivatives contracts. Therefore, the complexity of owning and managing structured securities can and should be addressed through an understanding of derivatives transactions and their risks.

By their nature, OTC derivatives are most frequently offered to institutional investors. It is possible, however, that unsophisticated individual investors might be offered complex structured securities. Protection of individual investors is the domain of national regulators who determine how offerings of all securities, including structured securities, can lawfully be made.

Financial Institutions Over 83% of the financial institutions responding to the Survey as end-users consider derivatives either very important (25%) or imperative (58%) for controlling risk within their organizations. Of the institutions responding, 92% use interest rate swaps, 54% use FRAs, 46% use currency swaps, 85% use cross-currency rate swaps, and 69% use forward foreign exchange contracts. In terms of option-based derivatives, 69% use interest rate options while 23% use currency options.

It should not be surprising that financial institutions consider derivatives important in managing their risk exposures. The volatile interest rates of the early 1980s dramatically increased the interest rate risk exposure of financial institutions such as commercial banks, mortgage banks, and insurance companies.

The effect of a change in interest rates on the market value of a financial institution's net worth depends on the relative interest rate sensitivities of its assets and liabilities, taking into account such factors as prepayment options in mortgages. The net worth of these institutions is vulnerable to changes in interest rates and shifts in the yield curve, because their assets and liabilities have different maturities and repricing characteristics.

Financial institutions typically manage their interest rate risk through an asset/liability management function. Derivatives are used widely in asset/liability management because of their versatility and efficiency. These institutions also use derivatives in conjunction with financings.

Managing a Bank's Investments Using Interest Rate Floors: *First Union Bank, a regional bank in the southeastern United States, uses derivatives to actively manage the investment side of its balance sheet and its overall interest rate risk. In 1991, for example, First Union Bank bought an interest rate floor giving it the right to receive 6.5% minus three-month LIBOR on $1 billion for five years. First Union Bank paid a $3 million premium for the floor. The floor protected the earnings on First Union Bank's assets from a decline in interest rates. By February of 1992, in fact, interest rates had fallen so far that First Union Bank was able to sell the floor for $30 million, which offset in part the reduced earnings on its investments over the life of the floor. See* United States Banker, *August 1992.*

Global derivatives are now used widely by financial institutions to manage the interest rate and foreign exchange risk arising from a variety of activities. Eighty-four percent of the financial institutions responding to the Survey indicate that they use derivatives for hedging market risks arising from new financings, 77% use them to manage their existing assets and liabilities, 39% use them to offset option positions embedded in the institution's assets and liabilities, 39% use them to hedge transaction exposures, and 46% use them to hedge translation exposures.

Dealers
The Function of Dealers Early in the evolution of OTC derivatives, financial institutions – including investment banks, commercial banks, merchant banks, and independent broker/dealers – acted for the most part as brokers finding counterparties with offsetting requirements with regard to notional amount, currencies, type of interest to be paid, frequency of payments, and maturity. They then negotiated on behalf of the two parties. Acting as agent or broker for a fee, the institutions took no principal position in the transactions and, hence, were not exposed to credit or market risk.

Most financial institutions found their role soon evolved beyond brokering to acting as dealers, offering themselves as counterparties or principals to intermediate customers' requirements. Transactions, however, were immediately matched or hedged by entering into an opposing transaction such as a "matched swap." Each pair of transactions was dealt with separately and discretely. As a result, the dealer's book of business was relatively simple to monitor and manage. This new role, however, required a commitment of capital since dealers now faced credit risk and some limited market risk.

The next step in the evolution of dealer activities was the "warehousing" of derivatives transactions. Dealers would temporarily hedge a swap – typically with a cash security or futures position – until a matched transaction could be found to replace the temporary hedge. This advance in risk management practice increased the ability of dealers to accommodate customer needs.

Today, major dealers have moved from the "warehouse" approach to a "portfolio" approach, wherein the dealer simply takes the customer's transaction into its portfolio or book of derivatives and manages the net or residual risk of its overall position. Each new transaction is decomposed into its component cash flows and risk factors and aggregated with all previous transactions. The focus of risk management changes from individual transactions to portfolio exposures. This has led to a marked improvement in the ability of dealers to accommodate a broad spectrum of customer transactions, and has improved their ability to monitor and manage the various components of market risk, regardless of the transactions from which the risks derive.

By quoting bid and offer prices, dealers provide liquidity and continuous availability of derivatives transactions. To supply the immediacy demanded by end-users, dealers use their own inventory, or establish new positions, and manage the resulting risk. They are compensated by earning a return from a bid-ask spread. In addition, dealers can take market risk positions to express market views in the expectation of profiting from favorable movements in prices or rates.

Dealers also provide an arbitrage function, identifying and exploiting anomalies between derivatives and underlying cash market instruments, thereby enhancing market liquidity and pricing efficiency. Finally, dealers earn a return for the amount of financial engineering that goes into developing customized and structured transactions that meet specific customer needs.

Types of Dealers Dealing in derivatives has tended to concentrate among principals possessing not only the requisite technology and know-how but also ample capital and credit appraisal experience. Banks have become the dominant derivatives players, but they hold no monopoly.[11] Securities firms, insurance companies, and high-rated corporates (especially in the energy area) are deploying capital and credit experience to run swap books to profit from both dealing and position-taking activity.

---

[11] Based on a ranking in *The World's Major Swap Dealers* (Swaps Monitor Publications, Inc., November 1992) for year-end 1991, 19 of the top 25 dealers in interest rate and currency swaps were banks; four were securities firms; and two were insurance companies. Out of the 25 dealers from around the world, 14 were U.S. based. Of the top 25 dealers in foreign exchange forwards, 24 were banks, while one was a securities firm.

The credit standing of the dealer is very important. Several dealers have created special purpose derivatives product companies which benefit from the support of a strong parent or shareholder. Some dealers have established separately capitalized, triple-A rated, derivatives vehicles.

III. Assessing and Managing the Risks of Derivatives

The risks to end-users and dealers involved in derivatives can be broadly categorized as market, credit, operational, and legal. These risks are of the same types that banks and securities firms have faced in their traditional lines of business – taking deposits and making loans, or purchasing and financing securities positions. The risks of derivatives, in other words, are not new. The management of derivatives activities, however, is more complex than it is for some of the traditional banking products. For derivatives activities, dealers have developed sophisticated risk management systems.

Some other banking products, such as residential mortgages with prepayment options, require a similarly sophisticated approach to risk management. An important by-product of derivatives activities has been that the knowledge dealers have gained about the assessment and management of risk has flowed out of derivatives groups into other areas, improving the general risk management techniques and policies of many firms. The assessment and management of the risks associated with derivatives activities is discussed below.

Market Risk

The market risk of derivatives, like that of any other financial instrument, depends upon their price behavior when market conditions change. In order to explain this behavior a dealer or end-user must identify the components of market risk and understand their interaction. The assessment of market risk relies on a mark-to-market valuation of derivatives and the underlying instruments which may serve as hedges.

A Portfolio Approach to Managing Market Risk Dealers now typically manage the market risks of their derivatives activity on the basis of the net or residual exposure of the overall portfolio. A dealer's portfolio generally will contain many offsetting positions, which substantially reduce the overall risk of the portfolio, leaving a much smaller residual risk to be hedged.

When managing market risk, a dealer first must determine properly the net position of the portfolio. Dealers look beyond the particular contracts and focus instead on identifying the fundamental risks they contain so the overall portfolio can be decomposed into underlying risk factors that can be quantified and managed. The fundamental risks that must be identified include:

- *Absolute price or rate (or delta) risk* This is the exposure to a change in the value of a transaction or portfolio corresponding to a given change in the price of an underlying.[12]

- *Convexity (or gamma) risk* This is the risk that arises when the relationship between the price of an underlying and the value of a transaction or portfolio is not linear. The greater the non-linearity (i.e., convexity) the greater the risk.[13]

- *Volatility (or vega) risk* This is typically associated with options and is the exposure to a change in the value of a transaction or portfolio resulting from a given change in the expected volatility of the price of an underlying.

- *Time decay (or theta) risk* This is typically associated with options and is the exposure to a change in the value of a transaction or portfolio arising from the passage of time.

- *Basis or correlation risk* This is the exposure of a transaction or portfolio to differences in the price performance of the derivatives it contains and their hedges.

- *Discount rate (or rho) risk* This is the exposure to a change in the value of a transaction or portfolio corresponding to a change in the rate used for discounting future cash flows.

Each of the six risks outlined above is measured across the different maturities (i.e., across the term structure) of the derivatives in the portfolio.

Once a portfolio has been decomposed into its component parts, the various risks can be aggregated and managed on a net basis.

Identifying the Risks of Individual Derivatives The market risks of a derivatives portfolio are best analyzed in terms of the fundamental risks associated with the two basic types of derivatives it may contain: forward-based and option-based derivatives. The fundamental risks of both types of transactions are outlined below.

Forward-Based Derivatives The market risks of forward-based derivatives are relatively straightforward since the dominant risk is absolute price or rate risk. Changes in the price of the underlying result in proportional changes in the value of the derivative. Forward-based derivatives generally do not have significant exposure to

---

[12] The delta of a single transaction can also be interpreted as the "equivalent position" in the underlying. That is, a portfolio composed, say, of an option and a position in the underlying, opposite to but the same size as the equivalent position, is said to be "delta hedged." Delta is a quantity that varies between zero and one. A swap would typically have a delta of about one. An option with a strike price set at the forward rate would have a delta of about one-half.

[13] Convexity or gamma risk is measured by the expected change in the delta of a single transaction or a portfolio in response to a change in the price of an underlying. Since gamma is the expected change in delta, it provides a measure of the expected change in the equivalent position with a change in price.

convexity (gamma) risk. The simplicity of the market risk profile of these derivatives makes hedging and monitoring risk easier than for option-based derivatives. A hedge will consist of a proportional amount of the underlying (or another forward-based derivative) and this hedge is, for all intents and purposes, relatively static.

Option-Based Derivatives The risks inherent in option-based derivatives are more complex. The valuation of options is based upon a set of theories and mathematical models built on foundations first developed in the 1970s. One of the key contributions was the option valuation model developed by Fisher Black and Myron Scholes. The Black-Scholes model identifies five factors that determine the value of many options: (i) the price of the underlying; (ii) the exercise price of the option; (iii) the time to expiration of the option; (iv) the volatility of the price of the underlying; and (v) the discount rate over the life of the option. These risk factors are considered below.

The relationship between the price of an option and the price of its underlying is not constant, as is the case with forward-based derivatives. For instance, if the value of the option changes by 50% of the change in the price of the underlying at a given price of the underlying, it may change by 70% at a different price. Therefore, the price sensitivity of an option's value changes with changes in the price of the underlying, so that options create exposures to the risk of gaps in prices of the underlying as well as directional movements. Options also create exposure to volatility risk. Changes in the expected volatility of the underlying will affect the value of the option, even if the price of the underlying remains constant. The passage of time also affects the value of an option because of time decay – the reduction in the likelihood that the option will end up in-the-money (or further in-the-money) as the time to expiration is reduced.

Dynamic Hedging The dynamic nature of the relationship between an option and the underlying is extremely important to risk managers in developing hedging strategies' for option-based derivatives. Since the price sensitivity of an option varies with changes in the price of the underlying, a position that is initially delta hedged must be adjusted as time passes or prices change if it is to remain hedged. The process of continuously hedging an option with a position in the underlying is known as "dynamic hedging."

Consider a financial institution that is delta hedging, for example, a short (or written) call option on a bond using a long position in the underlying bond. If the market rallies, the delta of the call option will increase and the hedge position in the underlying bond must be increased by buying additional amounts at higher prices in order to remain delta hedged. Although initially delta hedged, the position will incur some loss, the magnitude of the loss depending on the size of the price move and the convexity of the position. Failure to adjust the hedge also exposes the position to additional losses if the market continues to move up.

Hedging option-based derivatives is therefore a dynamic process, unlike the static hedging strategies of forward-based derivatives. If, instead of being short an option, a dealer is long an option, then the dynamic hedging process will result in gains every time the hedge is adjusted. The dealer will profit if actual volatility provides sufficient opportunity to realize dynamic gains relative to the volatility priced into the premium paid by the dealer.

There are two main risks associated with a dynamic hedge. The cost of hedging may turn out to be greater than expected because actual volatility is greater than expected; and the hedge does not protect completely against gapped markets and prices may move significantly before positions can be adjusted.

The alternative to the dynamic hedging of an options portfolio is to use options as hedges. The hedging of an option with another option is sometimes called gamma or vega hedging. Here the risks to changes in delta and changes in volatility are neutralized by offsetting changes in other options.

As with forwards, option-based derivatives of similar asset classes also are aggregated and managed as a group or book. Dealers tend to run balanced portfolios, hedging options with options, while dynamically hedging the smaller residual risk arising from mismatches in the options portfolio.

Market Liquidity Market liquidity risk is typically associated with the possibility that a large transaction in a particular instrument could have a discernible effect on the price of the instrument. This market impact effect increases the cost of hedging. In illiquid markets, moreover, bid-ask spreads are likely to be larger, further increasing that cost. A related phenomenon is the risk of an unexpected and sudden erosion of liquidity, possibly as a result of a sharp price move or jump in volatility.

By breaking the market risk of a particular product down into its fundamental elements, however, dealers are able to move beyond *product* liquidity to *risk* liquidity. For example, the interest rate risk of a complicated U.S. dollar interest rate swap can be hedged with other swaps, FRAs, Eurodollar futures contracts, treasury notes, or even bank loans and deposits. The customized swap may appear to be illiquid but, if its component risks are not, then other dealers can effectively acquire the transaction and hedge it.

Basis or Correlation Risk When a derivatives transaction is used to hedge another position, changes in the market value of the combined position result from basis risk. With a perfect hedge, the value of the combined position remains unchanged for a change in the price of the underlying. With an imperfect hedge, the values of the instrument and its hedge are not perfectly correlated. For example, when similar asset classes are aggregated so the risk can be managed on a portfolio basis, there may be maturity mismatches among deals or variation in price movements between the net derivatives position and the corresponding hedge. Correlation risk is an additional element of market risk that must be measured and managed.

Investing and Funding Risk Dealers and other participants who manage a portfolio of derivatives must meet the investing and funding requirements arising from cash flow mismatches. In addition, participants may be exposed to additional investing and funding requirements if the agreements they use to document transactions contain collateral provisions that produce cash and securities receipts or payments. The magnitude and direction of net cash positions can be forecast, but will fluctuate with changes in the market and activity in the portfolios. Transactions can be undertaken in derivatives and the cash markets to manage investing and funding risks.

Credit Risk

Credit risk is the risk that a loss will be incurred if a counterparty defaults on a derivatives contract. The loss due to a default is the cost of replacing the contract with a new one. The replacement cost at the time of default is equal to the present value of the expected future cash flows.

Credit Risk of Individual Derivatives The credit risk of a derivatives transaction fluctuates over time with the underlying variables that determine the value of the contract. In assessing credit risk, one needs to ask the following two questions: If a counterparty was to default today, what would it cost to replace the transaction? If a counterparty defaults at some point in the future, what is a reasonable estimate of the potential replacement cost? These two questions can be restated as: What is the "current" exposure? What is the "potential" exposure?

Current Exposure The first question is straightforward, since it simply asks for the current market value of the derivative at a given point in time – the cost of replacing the remaining cash flows at the prices and market interest rates prevailing when the event of termination occurs. The replacement cost could be positive or negative, depending on the evolution of the underlying since the inception of the transaction. Whenever the replacement cost is negative, the remaining party incurs no loss if its counterparty defaults.

Potential Exposure The second question is more difficult to answer, in that it calls for an assessment of what the replacement cost of the derivatives transaction could be in the future if the underlying variables that determine the value of the contract move adversely. Dealers use Monte Carlo or historical simulation studies or option valuation models to assess potential exposure. These analyses generally involve modeling the volatility of the underlying and the effect of its movements on the value of the derivatives transaction. These techniques are often used to generate two measures of potential exposure: "expected" exposure and maximum or "worst case" exposure.

Expected exposure at any point during the life of the swap is the mean of all possible replacement costs, where the replacement cost in any outcome is equal to the market value, if positive, and zero, if negative. Loosely speaking, expected exposure is the best estimate of the present value of the positive exposure, or credit risk, that is likely to materialize. As such, expected exposure is an important measure in derivatives dealers' capital allocation and pricing decisions.

Expected loss can be calculated statistically by combining the expected exposure and the probability of default.

The maximum potential exposure is calculated as an estimate of "worst case" exposure at any point in time. These calculations are based on adverse movements in the underlying variables that are sufficiently extreme that they are unlikely to be exceeded. For example, maximum potential exposure may be calculated so that there is statistically only a 5% chance that the actual exposure will be greater than the calculated maximum exposure. This "worst case" exposure is important in assessing the maximum amount that could possibly be at risk to a given counterparty and, as such, is important in dealers' credit allocation decisions.

It is important to appreciate that counterparty default in a forward or swap transaction may not cause a loss. For a credit loss to occur on a forward or swap transaction, two conditions must coexist – that the counterparty defaults *and* that the replacement cost of the transaction (i.e., the exposure) is positive.[14]

Unlike forwards and swaps, counterparty risk in options is one-sided. The buyer of the option typically pays in full for the option at contract initiation. The seller, however, is not required to perform until the option is exercised. This exposes the buyer to credit risk in that the seller may default prior to fulfilling the commitment under the option.

Credit Risk of a Portfolio The discussion to this point has dealt with the credit exposure for a single derivatives transaction. It is extremely important, although more complex, to obtain an accurate assessment of the total credit exposure on a portfolio of transactions with the same counterparty.

In calculating the current replacement costs for a portfolio of transactions with a counterparty, it is important to know whether netting applies and is enforceable. Master agreements used for documenting swaps typically provide for netting of close-out values across all transactions under the contract in the event of default. If a counterparty defaults, application of close-out netting will result in all the outstanding transactions being terminated and marked to market; the net (not gross) amount owed under all the transactions would be the replacement cost for that counterparty. If netting applies, the current credit exposure is simply the sum of the positive and negative mark-to-market values of the transactions in the portfolio. If netting does not apply, only the positive mark-to-market transactions should be added in calculating current exposure because the positive mark-to-market positions could not be offset against negative mark-to-market positions in the event of default.

The potential exposure for a portfolio of transactions is more difficult to calculate. While the simplest method is to add the potential exposure of each transaction in the portfolio, this procedure dramatically overstates, in most cases, the actual potential exposure. It does not take into account transactions in the portfolio with offsetting exposures or transactions that have peak maximum potential exposures that occur at different times. The potential exposure of a portfolio of transactions with a given counterparty can be analyzed more thoroughly by portfolio-level simulation that

---

[14] This is in contrast to the one-sided credit exposure of a loan. Default on a loan requires only that the borrower be in financial distress. Moreover, the creditor faces default risk on interest payments and the unamortized principal of a loan throughout its life. In a forward or swap, the notional principal generally is not at risk. This is not true for the principal of a loan. These differences explain why the impact of credit differentials on swap spreads are much smaller than on loans.

accounts for portfolio effects and provides more accurate measures of expected and maximum potential exposure than would be obtained by aggregating exposures on individual transactions.

The overall credit risk of a derivatives portfolio also depends upon the extent of diversification across specific counterparties and types of counterparties. For large diversified derivatives portfolios, "worst case" exposure becomes a less useful measure since it is highly unlikely that all worst case outcomes will occur simultaneously. Concentration of the portfolio with one counterparty (or type of counterparty) increases credit risk. This is as true for a derivatives portfolio as it is for a loan book.

Managing Credit Risk Dealers adopt policies and procedures to manage counterparty credit risk including: internal controls that ensure that credit risk is assessed prior to entering into transactions with a given counterparty and that credit risk is monitored over the life of the transaction; documentation provisions that mitigate credit risk and ensure transaction enforceability; and credit enhancement structures that further reduce or limit the credit exposure of dealing with particular counterparties.

The credit risk in these derivatives is addressed generally through counterparty credit evaluation and by the use of risk limits for counterparties. The credit quality of the users of global derivatives is typically high. For less creditworthy counterparties, credit enhancement methods such as collateral are often employed.

Although the measurement of credit exposures for derivatives transactions is more complicated than the measurement of exposure for more traditional banking products, the principles of assuming credit risk and managing these risks remain the same. For this reason, major dealers typically manage credit exposure on a consistent and integrated basis across the organization. Specifically, the evaluation of the credit exposures of derivatives transactions is made on a comparable basis with those exposures for on-balance-sheet activities, allowing the dealer to consistently integrate the two activities in the credit allocation and review process.

For many banks, derivatives (especially swaps) represent an excellent source of credit assets. Since derivative counterparties are often borrowers in the public markets, they are generally investment grade risks. Therefore, as they write swaps, financial intermediaries take credit exposure to exactly those high-grade sovereign and corporate clients that they prefer, but which rarely appear in loan books. For lending institutions, swaps appear to have increased the average quality and the diversity of the credit risks to which the firm is exposed.

Settlement Risk One aspect of settlement risk results from the fact that few financial transactions are settled on a same-day basis, or simultaneously. In the U.S. equity markets, for example, the difference between the trade date and settlement is at present five days. As a result, one party could suffer a loss if the price moved in his favor and the counterparty refused to exchange on the settlement date.[15] The largest settlement exposures, however, typically occur on the settlement day itself when the full

---

[15] This two-sided settlement risk is, of course, similar to the two-sided credit risk of forwards and swaps.

value of the security can be at risk if delivery of the security and delivery of the payment are not synchronized.

Settlement risk in derivatives is reduced greatly by the widespread use of the payment netting provisions of master agreements. This reduces the settlement risk of payments made in the same currency. In addition, for many derivative transactions (e.g., interest rate swaps), principal amounts are not exchanged on the maturity date.

Payment netting, however, does not address cross currency settlement risk. The largest source of settlement risk in payment systems is the settlement exposure created by foreign currency trades – spot and short-dated forwards – (called "Herstatt" risk after the 1974 failure of the Bankhaus Herstatt). While derivatives activity would benefit from a reduction of Herstatt risk, it must be noted that the amounts involved in derivatives are very small relative to the amounts involved in traditional foreign exchange activities. It has been estimated by ISDA that daily global cash flows from interest rate swaps and currency swaps average $0.65 billion and $1.9 billion, respectively. In contrast, the BIS Central Bank Survey of Foreign Exchange Market Activity in April 1992 estimated daily global net turnover in foreign exchange spot and forward markets at $400 billion and $420 billion, respectively.

Operational Risk

Operational risk is the risk of losses occurring as a result of inadequate systems and control, human error, or management failure. Such risks also exist in securities and credit businesses. The complexity of derivatives, however, requires special emphasis on maintaining adequate human and systems controls to validate and monitor the transactions and positions of dealers. The main types of internal controls, depending upon the level of derivatives and the sophistication of the institution, may include the following:

- Oversight of informed and involved senior management.

- Documentation of policies and procedures, listing approved activities and establishing limits and exceptions, credit controls, and management reports.

- Independent risk management function (analogous to credit review and asset/liability committees) that provides senior management validation of results and utilizations of limits.

- Independent internal audits which verify adherence to the firm's policies and procedures.

- A back office with the technology and systems for handling confirmations, documentation, payments, and accounting.

- A system of independent checks and balances throughout the transaction process, from front-office initiation of a trade to final payment settlement.

Legal Risk

Legal risk is the risk of loss because a contract cannot be enforced. This includes risks arising from insufficient documentation, insufficient capacity or authority of a counterparty (*ultra vires*), uncertain legality, and unenforceability in bankruptcy or insolvency.

Although financial institutions have encountered these legal risks in their traditional lending and trading businesses, the risks come in new forms with derivatives. Legal analysis of derivatives-related disputes, moreover, often turns on form as well as substance. In the early days of global derivatives activity, lawyers were presented with a host of issues – corporate, constitutional, tax, regulatory – that grew out of the fact that existing laws and regulations had been written before these new transactions were developed.

In numerous contexts derivatives lawyers have dealt with two basic questions: What is it? How does it fit into a given legislative or regulatory scheme? Many of these questions have been answered through better understanding of the economics of derivatives and the nature of various specific derivatives transactions. Widely used standard documentation also has eased legal concerns in many jurisdictions. Changes in the legal environment in various jurisdictions also have answered certain specific enforceability issues. Nevertheless, there remain legal issues related to enforceability that need to be clarified in order to reduce enforceability risk.

Illegality/Unenforceability Enforceability risk results from the possibility that a derivatives contract with a positive replacement cost might be found to be unenforceable. This might result from one's counterparty being legally incapable of entering into the contract (i.e., *ultra vires*) or from an entire class of contracts being declared illegal or unenforceable.

Ultra Vires: *In January 1991, the U.K. House of Lords held that the London Borough of Hammersmith and Fulham lacked the necessary capacity to enter into interest rate swap contracts it had entered into during the 1980s, and therefore was not liable to make payments on those contracts on which it would otherwise have suffered large losses. The losses suffered by swap dealers as a result of this decision are estimated to represent over 50% of total losses due to defaults on swaps since the inception of swap activity.*[16] *The Local Government Act 1972, from which local authorities derive their powers, does not include any express power for local authorities to enter into derivatives transactions and the House of Lords found no implied powers whether for hedging purposes or otherwise. Prior to the House of Lords decision, the question of the capacity of local authorities to enter into swaps had been discussed with certain regulatory bodies and with legal counsel, and a not uncommon view was that local authorities had the capacity to enter into swaps as a risk management tool in certain circumstances.*

---

[16] The decision emphasizes the desirability of clear legal authority as to the capacity of parties to enter into derivatives transactions.

Exchange-Trading Requirement: *In the United States, a major source of legal risk has been the exchange-trading requirement for futures in the Commodity Exchange Act (CEA).[17] The terms "commodity," "futures," and "options" have been broadly interpreted by the Commodity Futures Trading Commission (CFTC), creating concerns that OTC derivatives such as swaps could be found to be illegal off-exchange futures contracts. In an Advance Notice of Proposed Rulemaking in 1987, the CFTC questioned the legality of the newly emerging commodity swap market, driving commodity swap activity offshore. This view was reversed in July 1989 when the CFTC released a Policy Statement stating that swaps were not appropriately regulated as futures contracts and providing a non-exclusive safe harbor for swaps satisfying·certain conditions. With the passage of the Futures Trading Practices Act of 1992, the CFTC was given explicit authority to exempt swaps from regulation under the CEA. In January 1993, the CFTC used this new exemptive authority to clarify the status of swaps and greatly reduce the legal risk that swaps with U.S. counterparties would be found to be illegal off-exchange futures contracts.*

Close-Out Netting and Insolvency Provisions for netting of exposures on transactions documented under master agreements offer obvious benefits to end-users and dealers. Doubts exist, however, in some quarters and jurisdictions about the enforceability of such close-out netting provisions. First, there is the possibility that a bankruptcy trustee or liquidator could attempt to cherry-pick among the swaps documented under a master agreement, enforcing only those that have positive value to the party in bankruptcy or liquidation. Second, there are some obstacles to immediate termination of swaps when a default takes place. For example, in some countries, the relevant legislation contains an automatic stay provision which could prevent immediate termination on bankruptcy or liquidation, creating uncertainty about whether termination will be permitted and, if permitted, what the termination value will be.

IV. The Level of Activity and Risk Exposure of Derivatives

Measures of Activity and Risk
Measuring Activity Activity in OTC derivatives generally has been measured in two ways: by the total notional principal of contracts, either the amount outstanding at a particular time (e.g., year-end) or the amount written during a particular period (e.g., annually or quarterly); and by the number of transactions. These measures provide a rough but nevertheless useful measure of the level of activity in derivatives, both in the aggregate and at the individual firm level.

In using notional principal as a measure of activity in derivatives, care must be taken to account for doublecounting of some activity. Depending upon the source of the data, that doublecounting may be substantial. For example, when swap activity of

---

[17] In *Transnor (Bermuda) Ltd. v. B.P. North America Petroleum*, a federal court found in 1990 that the forward market in Brent crude oil was a United States futures market. Since the market was not designated by the Commodity Futures Trading Commission as a contract market, transactions in this market could have been construed as illegal off-exchange futures contracts. Losing counterparties could potentially have walked away from the contracts without meeting their obligations.

U.S. banks is derived from call reports, there is substantial doublecounting since many of the swap contracts outstanding at one bank will have other U.S. banks as counterparties. The International Swaps and Derivatives Association (ISDA) in its regular survey of swap activity of its members has recognized this and adjusts for doublecounting by dividing the figures for total transactions between dealers by two. The doublecounting problem explains in part why the use of different sources frequently results in different measures of the overall level of activity in derivatives.

Data on derivatives activities is often collected both in terms of outstandings at a point in time, and as new activity generated during a specific period. Notional activity generated in a specified time period may better reflect market activity since changes in amounts outstanding are due both to new activity and the maturing or cancellation of existing transactions.

Data on derivatives activity is collected primarily by private industry groups, as well as by regulators in the normal course of their supervisory process (e.g., bank call reports in the United States). In addition, as more dealers and end-users report derivatives activity with increased levels of detail in their public accounts, data can be consolidated from a review of the public reports of firms involved in this area. Industry groups include ISDA, which is a global organization representing all types of dealers. Several national banking organizations, such as the Association Française des Banques, the Australian Financial Markets Association, and the British Bankers Association, have also collected data on localized segments of derivatives activity.

Given the breadth of the membership of ISDA, its data is the most comprehensive, and is used extensively as a reference by both market participants and regulators. ISDA has collected data on a consistent basis since 1985 and, as mentioned, adjusts its figures to eliminate the effects of doublecounting of transactions between dealers. Beginning with U.S. dollar interest rate swaps in 1985, ISDA added interest rate and currency swaps in the full range of major currencies in 1987, and caps, floors, collars, and swap options in 1989. Group of Thirty support helped ISDA extend coverage of its statistics to equity, commodity, and multi-asset derivatives. The results at year-end 1992 are summarized in Table 5.

These measures of notional principal, it is important to note, do not measure the risk exposures associated with derivatives. Other measures must be used for meaningful readings on risk exposures.

Measuring Risk The most accurate measure of credit risk at a point in time is provided by the net replacement cost of a derivatives portfolio – the cost of replacing the remaining cash flows of the derivatives at prevailing interest rates and exchange rates.

Notional principal outstanding cannot be used as a measure of risk exposure (either credit or market risk) for three main reasons. First, notional principal outstanding fails to account for offsetting exposures.[18] Second, transactions of various maturities are simply added together without accounting for the differing sensitivities of the values of the contracts to changes in the value of the underlying (e.g., the interest rate risk of a one-year interest rate swap is not equal to that of a ten-year swap even if the notional principals are the same). Finally, different types of derivatives (e.g., interest rate versus currency swaps) have substantially different risk profiles. For these same reasons, figures on new contracts written cannot be used as a measure of risk exposures.

The Level, Growth, and Composition of Derivatives Activity

ISDA survey data provides the most comprehensive and consistent data set for measuring the level, growth, and composition of derivatives activity. The survey data is based on the responses of ISDA's members, capturing the vast bulk of activity in most sectors, and is adjusted for doublecounting.

Interest Rate and Currency Swaps As indicated in Table 2, the notional principal of interest rate plus currency swaps written in 1991 was $1.95 trillion, 32% more than in 1990 and a three-fold increase over 1987. Likewise, the notional principal of interest rate swaps written during 1991 was $1.62 trillion, four times the amount written in 1987. Currency swaps written during 1991 were $328 billion, somewhat less than three times the amount written in 1987. Table 2 also shows that, for year-end 1991, the notional principal outstanding of interest rate plus currency swaps was $3.87 trillion, or three and a half times the year-end 1987 outstanding of $867 billion.[19]

Table 3 provides information on the composition of swap activity by type of counterparty. Of the $1.95 trillion in interest rate and currency swaps written in 1991, $866 billion in notional principal or 44% involved transactions between dealers; $591 billion or 30% was between dealers and other financial institutions; $362 billion or 18.6% was between dealers and corporations; while $132 billion or 6.8% was between dealers and governments or other entities.

---

[18] Consider the following example. Suppose a bank enters into an interest rate swap with a corporation, paying a floating rate and receiving a fixed rate on $100 million of notional principal. At a later date, suppose the corporation decides to adjust its exposure by entering into another $100 million swap with the bank taking on the opposite interest rate exposure – the bank receives floating and pays fixed. A survey of the bank's swap book would now show $200 million in notional principal outstanding for this pair of transactions. This is so despite the fact that the economic exposures in the two swaps are offsetting. The same problem would apply if the corporation entered into the second swap with a different bank. A survey of the swap activity of all banks would count the two offsetting swaps as $200 million of notional principal outstanding. If, instead, the corporation had negotiated an unwind of the initial swap, the notional principal outstanding from the pair of transactions would be zero. As a result, notional principal outstanding can overstate the risk of exposure in derivatives.

[19] The table also breaks down the volume of swaps written annually by underlying currency.

Table 2
Interest Rate and Currency Swaps Written Annually by Underlying and Outstanding
(Notional Principal in Billions of U.S. Dollars: 1987-91)

Type of Swap	1987	1988	1989	1990	1991
Interest Rate Swaps					
US$	287	366	545	676	926
DM	22	33	41	106	103
Yen	32	43	62	137	194
Others	47	126	185	345	399
Subtotal	388	568	833	1,264	1,622
Currency Swaps					
Yen-Dollar	24	35	53	48	80
Others-Dollar	30	35	40	33	60
Non-Dollar	32	54	86	132	188
Subtotal	86	124	179	213	328
Total Swaps Written	474	692	1,012	1,477	1,950
Total Swaps Outstanding (at Year-End)	867	1,328	1,952	2,890	3,872

Source: International Swaps and Derivatives Association

Table 3
Interest Rate and Currency Swaps Written Annually by Type of Counterparty and Outstanding
(Notional Principal in Billions of U.S. Dollars: 1987-91)

Counterparty	1987	1988	1989	1990	1991
Transactions Between Dealers	144	222	368	546	865
Transactions With End-Users					
Financial Institutions	203	282	370	472	591
Corporations	86	127	186	286	362
Governments	35	52	63	98	111
Others	6	9	25	75	21
Subtotal	330	470	644	931	1,085
Total Swaps Written	474	692	1,012	1,477	1,950
Total Swaps Outstanding (at Year-End)	867	1,328	1,952	2,890	3,872

Source: International Swaps and Derivatives Association

Interest Rate Options Table 4 provides information on the composition of interest rate options outstanding by type of option – that is, cap, floor, collar, or swaption. At year-end 1991, the notional principal outstanding of these newer option-based derivatives was $317 billion for interest rate caps, 25% more than in 1989 but slightly less than in 1990; $129 billion for floors, 50% more than in 1989; $22 billion for collars, 44% less than in 1989; and $109 billion for swaptions, over 50% more than in 1989. The combined total for all four types of interest rate options was $578 billion. The total notional principal outstanding for these interest rate option-based derivatives amounts to 15% of interest rate and currency swaps outstanding as of year-end 1991.[20]

Table 4

Interest Rate Options:

Caps, Floors, Collars, and Swaptions Outstanding

(Notional Principal in Billions of U.S. Dollars: 1989-91)

Year-End	1989	1990	1991
Caps			
U.S.$	177	251	225
Non-U.S.$	77	68	92
Subtotal	254	319	317
Floors			
U.S.$	54	76	73
Non-U.S.$	32	34	56
Subtotal	86	110	129
Collars			
U.S.$	35	33	13
Non-U.S.$	4	5	10
Subtotal	39	38	23
Swaptions			
U.S.$	51	63	57
Non-U.S.$	21	31	52
Subtotal	72	94	109
Combined			
U.S.$	317	423	368
Non-U.S.$	134	138	210
Total	451	561	578

Source: International Swaps and Derivatives Association

[20] This is an overstatement of the real relative size since the option-based contracts are not converted to equivalent positions in the underlyings based on price or yield sensitivities.

Equity, Commodity, and Multi-Asset Derivatives In a recent survey, ISDA estimated for the first time the level of activity in equity and commodity swaps and options and in a new survey category of multi-asset transactions that have components indexed to two or more underlyings. The results of this survey are summarized in Table 5. At year-end 1992, the notional principal amounts of equity swaps and options outstanding were estimated to be $10 billion and $66 billion, respectively; commodity swaps and options were estimated to be $18 billion and $12 billion, respectively; while multi-asset transactions totaled $25 billion. The total notional principal amount of all these newly surveyed transactions combined is $131 billion, about 3% of the interest rate and currency swaps outstanding as of year-end 1991. When these transactions are combined with the interest rate options (i.e., caps, floors, collars, and swaptions) the total notional principal amount outstanding is $709 billion or 18% of swap activity.

Table 5

Equity, Commodity, and Multi-Asset Derivatives Outstanding at Year-End 1992
(Notional Principal in Billions of U.S. Dollars)

	Transactions Between Dealers	Transactions With End-Users	Total Outstanding
Commodity Swaps			
Energy	5	10	15
Metals	–	3	3
Subtotal	5	13	18
Commodity Options			
Energy	2	3	5
Metals	2	5	7
Subtotal	4	8	12
Equity Swaps			
Indices (by Index Country)			
Japan	3	3	6
U.S.	1	1	2
Other	–	1	1
Baskets and Individual Stocks	–	1	1
Subtotal	4	6	10
Equity Options			
Indices (by Index Country)			
Japan	11	9	20
U.S.	3	8	11
U.K.	6	5	11
Germany	4	2	6
France	3	2	5
Other	2	2	4
Baskets	–	2	2
Individual Stocks	1	6	7
Subtotal	30	36	66
Multi-Asset Transactions	10	15	25
Combined Total	53	78	131

Source: International Swaps and Derivatives Association

Comparison to Other Financial Activities While the numbers on new swaps written and swaps outstanding shown in Table 2 indicate a significant growth in overall swaps activity from 1987 to 1991, it is important to put these numbers in perspective. One obvious comparison is with the trading or turnover in exchange-traded markets for futures and options and the foreign exchange markets. In 1991, ISDA dealers reported writing 74,340 swaps with a notional principal of $1.95 trillion. In contrast, in 1992, more than 600 million futures and options contracts were traded on organized exchanges, representing a face value or notional amount exceeding $140 trillion.[21] Global net turnover in the foreign exchange markets, in April 1992, was estimated to have totalled $880 billion per day, or roughly $220 trillion on an annual basis.[22]

The size of OTC derivatives activity can be put into further perspective by comparing it with the activity in other selected global financial markets. This is done in Table 6 for year-end 1991. Swaps outstanding of $4.5 trillion (including caps, floors, collars, and swaptions, along with interest rates and currency swaps) is compared to bonds (domestic and cross-border) outstanding of $14.4 trillion and equities (domestic and cross-border) outstanding of $10.1 trillion.

Table 6

Global Financial Activity

(Outstandings in Trillions of U.S Dollars: Year-End 1991)

Selected Markets	Outstanding
Swaps	4.5
Bonds (Domestic and Cross-border)	14.4
Equities (Domestic and Cross-border)	10.1

The amount for swaps includes interest rate and currency swaps plus caps, floors, collars, and swaptions outstanding for year-end 1991. Equity, commodity, and multi-asset derivatives are not included. They totalled $131 billion year-end 1992.

Source: J.P. Morgan

The Level of Credit Exposure in Derivatives

The large size of total notional principal outstanding or written has led some regulators and others to express concern, if not alarm, about the risk being taken on by banks and others through derivatives. The underlying concern, of course, is that taxpayers will be left to pick up the bill for any excessive risk taking. As pointed out above, however, notional principal outstanding is not an appropriate measure of risk. In fact, it greatly overstates risk.

---

[21] See "The Recent Growth of Financial Derivatives Markets," Eli M. Romolona, *Quarterly Review* (Federal Reserve Bank of New York, Winter 1992-93).

[22] See "Central Bank Survey of Foreign Exchange Market Activity in April 1992," Bank for International Settlements, Basle, March 1993.

One commonly used measure of credit exposure is gross replacement cost. This measure, however, overstates credit exposure since it does not account for the netting of settlement amounts in the event of default. Counterparties may have obligations that are at least partially offsetting. For example, a counterparty might owe a bank $20 million under one currency swap, while the bank owes the counterparty $12 million under another currency swap. The net exposure of $8 million is much less than the gross exposure of $20 million on the first contract. In the event of default, the net exposure is the relevant number for measuring credit risk where master agreements provide for the bilateral netting of close-out values across all transactions under the contract and the netting provisions are enforceable.

Whether measured on a gross or net basis, the replacement cost of a derivatives portfolio is likely to be a small percentage (i.e., 1% to 3%) of the total notional principal of the portfolio. An estimate of the gross replacement cost of United States banks' OTC derivatives portfolios is provided in Table 7. The gross replacement cost as of year-end 1992 for all such derivatives positions of these 50 leading banks was $144.0 billion – $49.7 billion in replacement costs for interest rate contracts and $94.3 billion for currency contracts. This is less than the replacement cost for year-end 1991. The total replacement cost of $144.0 billion represents less than 11% of the market value of the assets of these banks and 120% of their total capital. Replacement costs as a percentage of total notional principal outstanding was 1.61% for interest rate contracts and 2.98% for currency contracts, resulting in an average of 2.30% for all of these OTC derivatives contracts.[23]

Table 7
Derivatives Exposure by Lead Banks of 50 Largest U.S. Bank Holding Companies
(Year-End 1990-1992)

Gross Replacement Costs

Year	*Interest Rate Contracts* $ Billion	Percent of Notional Principal	*Currency Contracts* $ Billion	Percent of Notional Principal	*Combined Exposure* $ Billion
1990	26.2	1.15	76.3	2.82	102.5
1991	47.8	1.61	99.4	3.70	147.2
1992	49.7	1.61	94.3	2.98	144.0

The gross replacement cost is the mark-to-market value for OTC derivatives contracts with positive replacement cost, including swaps, forwards, purchased options, when-issued securities, and forward deposits accepted. Exchange-traded contracts and foreign exchange contracts with less than 14 days maturity are excluded.

Source: Consolidated Reports of Condition and Income.

[23] The gross replacement cost of the currency contracts of $94.3 billion is due mainly to the exposure resulting from foreign exchange forward contracts instead of currency swaps. At year-end 1992, the notional value of foreign exchange forwards was 10 times the notional value of currency swaps outstanding at these banks.

It is also important to remember, as pointed out above, that gross replacement cost overstates credit risk; it ignores the netting of swap obligations in the event of default. According to estimates provided by the Federal Reserve System, netting of interest rate contracts and currency contracts would reduce credit exposure by roughly 40% to 60% relative to gross replacement costs.[24] Credit exposure would be reduced even further under cross-product netting.

Sources of Growth in Derivatives

The growth in derivatives activity documented above can be attributed to at least four major factors. First, the opportunity to lower funding costs and enhance yields through arbitrage opportunities was the driving force behind the early growth of global derivatives, especially swaps, and continues to be a major source of growth. This arbitrage-induced growth was promoted by, and in turn facilitated, the global trends toward greater market integration and efficiency.

Second, major shifts in exchange rate and interest rate volatility in the early and late 1970s, respectively, and more recent temporary surges in volatility (including surges in the volatility of commodity and equity prices) have increased the demand for market-risk-management products.

Third, a driving force on the supply side is the substantial and secular reduction in transaction costs that has been occurring over the last 15 years, due in part to ongoing advances in communication and information-processing technologies and in part to deregulation. The cost of implementing arbitrage, hedging, and other risk management strategies has been dramatically reduced.

Finally, intellectual breakthroughs in finance – starting with the development of option pricing models in the early 1970s and continuing with the ongoing development of new and refined valuation models and simultaneous techniques for derivatives – have allowed derivatives participants to more accurately price derivatives and assess and manage their risks. These developments have led to further growth in the offering and use of derivatives.

V. The Effects of Derivatives on the Financial System and the Economy

The rapid growth of global derivatives transactions has led some observers to question whether this activity might increase systemic risks in the financial markets or complicate the efforts of supervisors to deal with systemic disturbances. A complete evaluation of the contribution of derivatives to the economy must consider these potential consequences and assess their likelihood and significance. This section examines the systemic implications of derivatives activity and briefly assesses the impact of derivatives on the overall economy. (A more thorough discussion is contained in the Working Paper of the Systemic Issues Subcommittee appearing in Appendix I, published separately).

---

[24] Letter from Alan Greenspan, Chairman, Board of Governors of the Federal Reserve System, to Senator Donald Riegle, Jr., September 11, 1992.

Derivatives and Systemic Risk

Supervisory authorities, who have studied the systemic issues posed by derivatives, have defined systemic risk as "the risk that a disruption (at a firm, in a market segment, to a settlement system, etc.) causes widespread difficulties at other firms, in other market segments or in the financial system as a whole."[25] This definition makes it clear that systemic risk arises in the course of ordinary market activities. Therefore it may be difficult to eliminate without curtailing these activities.

There is no general agreement as to which aspects of derivatives activity pose the greatest systemic concerns. Relevant issues include: the size and complexity of derivatives activity; the concentration of activity among a relatively small number of institutions; the lack of transparency of risk management activities, including derivatives; the apparent illiquidity of customized derivatives transactions; increased settlement risk because of the growth of derivatives; the credit exposures undertaken by dealers; the presence, among large dealers, of unregulated activities; the interconnection risk arising from the role played by derivatives in increasing links among capital markets; and the legal risks associated with conducting a new activity in an old legal framework. What follows is a brief discussion of each topic from a practitioner's perspective.

Size and Complexity This Overview has described an activity that is large, but still modest in size relative to activities in other markets. Its complexity, which is a reflection of the equally complex risks in the real economy, would merit concern if it outstripped participants' ability to evaluate and manage the attendant risks. There is much evidence to the contrary, as the Survey of Industry Practice confirms. Most dealers have gone to great lengths to establish sophisticated techniques to manage their derivatives exposures with considerable precision; many are extending the benefits of these techniques.

Concentration The geographic diversity of dealers and the different types of institutions acting as dealers considerably reduce the level of concentration, both within countries and for a group of institutions (e.g., banks). A survey based on available data from annual reports of dealers indicates that the top eight dealers accounted for only 58% of the interest rate and currency swap markets at year-end 1991.[26] No firm in that survey had over a 10% share of the market. While only one indication of concentration, ISDA dealers number 150: this is three times the number of primary dealers in U.S. government bonds.

Lack of Transparency This is mentioned in the context of internal management reporting, external financial reporting, or the collection of industry data. As to the first aspect, the Survey suggests that many participants, especially dealers, mark their

---

[25] Source: *Recent Developments in Interbank Relations*, Report prepared by a Working Group established by the Central Banks of the Group of Ten countries, Bank for International Settlements, Basle, October 1992 (the "Promisel Report").

[26] Source: *The World's Major Swap Dealers*, Swaps Monitor Publications, Inc., November 1992.

derivatives positions to market for risk management purposes, an important step towards transparency. The recommendations set forth in this Study call on participants to follow a set of practices which ensure management awareness at all levels.

Financial reporting is one area where the institutional framework – here, accounting standards and reporting requirements – has not kept up with the development of derivatives. The recommendations call on participants to voluntarily adopt accounting and disclosure practices for international harmonization and greater transparency, pending the arrival of international standards.

As for industry data, private industry organizations have contributed substantially, and continue to do so, to the base of information and consolidated data that exists on OTC derivatives.

Illiquidity The liquidity of derivatives transactions has been successfully tested in several situations of failure by large participants. By moving from the management of individual positions to the management of components of market risk, derivatives dealers have been able to move beyond product liquidity to risk liquidity: a customized swap may appear to be illiquid, but if its component risks are liquid, then dealers will be willing to provide liquidity. Positions can become illiquid, however, particularly in a crisis.

Illiquidity can also be an issue for individual participants who hedge through a dynamic process. Those who are most exposed are those who have sold options and thus have short volatility and convexity positions. These risks can be hedged by buying options or by using dynamic hedging to cover any net remaining position. Dynamic hedging is not applied to an entire portfolio, but only to the uncovered risk.

Most dealers, the Survey indicates, have a healthy respect for illiquidity risk and take it into account in their risk limits or on a case-by-case basis. Stress testing is also employed.

Settlement Risk Relative to the settlement risk of foreign exchange transactions, which is very large given the volumes involved, the settlement risk of derivatives is modest. Such risk is further reduced for settlements in a single currency, by the netting provisions that are standard in derivatives contracts.

Credit Risk The amount of credit losses incurred in derivatives activities has been very low. In fact, the rate of credit losses in derivatives compared with loss rates for traditional banking products indicates that by participating in derivatives activity, bank dealers have increased the average credit quality and diversity of risk to which they are exposed. Study recommendations are designed to further reduce the level of credit risk by taking full advantage of netting provisions through the use of bilateral multi-product master agreements.

Unregulated Entities Unregulated entities – such as affiliates of U.S. broker-dealers or of insurance companies, and certain non-financial firms – have promoted competition and innovation without any evidence to date of increased risk to regulated dealers or increased systemic risk. Participants can evaluate for themselves the risks and benefits of trading with unregulated entities.

Market Linkages Derivatives have increased market linkages by intermediating markets efficiently and providing effective risk management tools to facilitate the operation of global businesses. At the same time there is concern that by fostering these linkages, derivatives make it possible for shocks to be transmitted faster and farther than was possible before. The academic research indicates that derivatives trading does not increase volatility in underlying markets.

Legal Risks Despite efforts to reduce legal risks, they remain significant and have the potential to create systemic problems. Large losses were sustained when the House of Lords made an *ultra vires* ruling on derivatives contracts entered into by U.K. local authorities (see page 51). The most serious enforceability issue is with bilateral close-out netting arrangements in bankruptcy. A Study recommendation urges regulators and supervisors to recognize netting where and to the full extent it is enforceable and to reflect these arrangements in their capital standards, thereby creating tangible incentives for use. More generally, participants must work with legislators and regulators to upgrade the legal framework to bring it in line with the development of derivatives.

While it is hard to find justification for the view that derivatives pose a greater systemic threat than other financial activities, there is no room for complacency. Once demystified, systemic concerns can best be addressed through: adherence to principles of good management practice, such as those laid out in the Study recommendations; reinforcement of the legal framework for the activity; improved accounting and disclosure standards; and cooperation between participants and official bodies towards a better understanding of the activity, its risk, and measures to mitigate them. These steps coincide with the conclusions of the Promisel Report.

The Impact on the Overall Economy

Financial economists have identified three ways in which financial innovation can increase the efficiency of the financial system and thereby improve the performance of the overall economy.[27] These are:

- By meeting investor and issuer demands for new securities and other financial products, expanding the opportunities for risk-sharing, risk-pooling, hedging, and intertemporal or spatial transfers of resources.

- By lowering transaction costs or increasing the liquidity of markets.

- By helping to solve costly contractual and informational problems.

---

[27] This section draws on "Financial Innovation and Economic Performance" by Robert C. Merton and "Financial Innovation: Achievements and Prospects" by Merton Miller. These articles appeared in the *Journal of Applied Corporate Finance*, Winter 1992.

These are precisely the forces behind the innovation and growth in derivatives over the past 15 years. Indeed, derivatives have:

- Expanded risk management capabilities and improved credit allocation by providing investors and issuers with a wide array of previously unavailable tools for managing risk exposures and raising capital.[28]

- Reduced the transaction costs of achieving desired risk profiles and increased the liquidity and pricing efficiency of international financial markets.

- Provided new tools for addressing contractual and informational problems.

The global nature, volume, and ubiquity of derivatives activity, as shown by the evidence presented in this Overview, make a contribution to the overall economy that may be difficult to quantify, but is nevertheless both favorable and substantial.

---

[28] Some critics have argued that derivatives activity is a "zero-sum game" – no value is created in the process. Although the payoffs from a derivatives transaction are zero-sum in the sense that the gain to one party equals the loss to the other, derivatives transactions can nevertheless create value, both individually and socially. By hedging, firms can reduce financial risks resulting from exposure to interest rate, exchange rate, or commodity price volatility, allowing management to focus on the firm's core business. Moreover, hedging can reduce a firm's total risk and the likelihood of financial distress. This benefits those owners, managers, employees, customers, and suppliers with a stake in the ongoing viability and health of the firm.

Group of Thirty Members

Group of Thirty Publications since 1985

Reports:

The Foreign Exchange Market in the 1980s
The Foreign Exchange Market Study Group. 1985

Countertrade in the World Economy
Robert V. Roosa, et al. 1985

Outlook for Mineral Commodities
R. H. Carnegie. 1986

Inflation Stabilization with Incomes Policy Support
Rudiger Dornbusch and Mario Henrique Simonsen, with discussion by Mario Brodersohn,
Michael Bruno, G. G. Johnson. 1987

Finance for Developing Countries
Richard A. Debs, David L. Roberts, Eli M. Remolona. 1987

International Macroeconomic Policy Co-ordination
Policy Co-ordination Study Group. 1988

Perestroika: A Sustainable Process for Change
John P. Hardt and Sheila N. Heslin, with commentary by Oleg Bogomolov. 1989

The Risks Facing the World Economy
The Risks Facing the World Economy Study Group. 1991

Financing Eastern Europe
Richard A. Debs, Harvey Shapiro and Charles Taylor. 1991

The Summit Process and Collective Security: Future Responsibility Sharing
The Summit Reform Study Group. 1991

Sea Changes in Latin America
Pedro Aspe, Andres Bianchi and Domingo Cavallo, with discussion by S.T. Beza and William
Rhodes. 1992

EMU After Maastricht
Peter B. Kenen. 1992

Special Reports:

Clearance and Settlement Systems in the World's Securities Markets
Steering & Working Committees of the Securities Clearance and Settlement Study. 1988

Clearance and Settlement Systems: Status Reports, Spring 1990
Various Authors. 1990

Conference on Clearance and Settlement Systems; London, March 1990: Speeches
Various Authors. 1990

Clearance and Settlement Systems: Status Reports, Year-End 1990
Various Authors. 1991

Clearance and Settlements Systems: Status Reports, Autumn 1992
Various Authors. 1992

Occasional Papers: